URBAN POLITICS:

THE POLITICAL CULTURE OF SUR 13 GANGS

REVISED EDITION

Rodrigo Ribera d'Ebre

THE STEAM PRESS PUBLISHING GROUP

www.thewestsiderblog.wordpress.com

Published by The Steam Press Publishing Group Inc.

P.O. Box 88077 Los Angeles, CA 90009-8077

First Published By Authorhouse 2006

ISBN- 13: 978-1480205024

Cover Design by: Cipriano Romo, Copyright© 2005

Printed in the United States of America 2013

ABOUT THE AUTHOR

Rodrigo Ribera d'Ebre is a Mexican American writer of short stories, novels, and essays. He was born in Los Angeles in 1976 to a working class family. He spent his adolescence surrounded by street crime, experiences which gave him an understanding of the complex urban environment. Thereafter, he graduated from California State University, Los Angeles with a degree in Political Science. Since then, he has devoted himself to literature. He lived in Latin America for four years and has traveled throughout North America, Latin America, and Europe. His influences include: Dostoyevsky, Camus, Kafka, Hobbes, Machiavelli, Rousseau, Foucault, and Mike Davis. He is the author of *The NAFTA Blueprint*, a political conspiracy thriller about the North American Union.

TABLE OF CONTENTS

PROLOGUE

Los Angeles County is made up of approximately eighty-eight incorporated cities which have merged into the county corporation. All of the incorporated cities have a city hall, however, not all of the incorporated cities have an official city seal or chamber of commerce, and many of these cities are either chartered or general-law cities. The difference between a chartered and a general-law city is that a chartered city has a written document similar to a constitution which grants the city legal powers and jurisdiction, while a general-law city has an unwritten constitution that is based on general principles and customs.

There are also forty unincorporated cities and forty-seven unincorporated communities within the Los Angeles County without a city hall, a chamber of commerce, an official seal, they are not general-law or chartered cities, and they have not merged into the county corporation.

Additionally, the city of Los Angeles is the largest municipality within the county corporation which houses ninety-one communities within its boundary which are divided into regional blocs.

The regional blocs include: San Fernando Valley, Westside/Beach/Los Angeles International Airport or LAX, Downtown/Central Los Angeles, Northeast Los Angeles, South Los Angeles/South Central, and the Harbor Area. Lastly, there are another thirty five communities within incorporated cities other than the city of Los Angeles.

Correspondingly, there are more than four hundred street gangs operating within the Los Angeles County jurisdiction which have adopted the boundaries and territory within the incorporated cities and the unincorporated communities. This statistically significant figure has merited the county of Los Angeles the title of "Gang Capital of the World." These organizations do not have a city hall, a chamber of commerce, or an official city seal; however they are all, to some extent, general-law communities which operate under general principles and customs.

These street gang general-law communities reflect the same function as a city or municipality in some factors such as: being centers of population, being centers of commerce, and maintaining a culture of some significant size and importance. Similar to the jurisdictions in the county corporation, these types of general-law communities adhere to the division of boundaries and regional blocs that make up the City and County of Los Angeles. Many of these street gangs operate within an incorporated city's boundaries; however, there are numerous communities and areas within these boundaries that have resisted the annexation of a larger gang in order to remain autonomous.

Los Angeles County's cosmopolitan population makes it a unique and highly distinct global region with an attractive social and cultural landscape; however, the harsh inequality and economic gap directly contribute to its paradoxical identity. The economic gap is so egregious that in many unincorporated communities, areas, and municipalities, the socio-economic status and the standard of living of its citizenry is comparable to that of underdeveloped countries. For example, the University of Southern California, which is one of the most prestigious, elite, and expensive universities in the world, is surrounded by one of the poorest neighborhoods in the county.

The University of Southern California is a private corporation located within the South Los Angeles regional bloc of the City of Los Angeles, which is also home to numerous street gangs. According to the 2008 U.S. News and World Report, the University of Southern California was ranked 27th amongst all national universities, with a notable alumni association, faculty, and research department.

The demographics surrounding the university are mostly made up of low-income Blacks, Hispanics, and recent immigrants, while the majority of the student body comes from white, middle-class suburban communities throughout the country. Moreover, demographic statistics demonstrate that approximately forty percent of the university students come from out-of-state, not the surrounding communities, with another eighteen percent associated with legacy preferences.

The University of Southern California is the largest private employer throughout the Los Angeles County, resulting mostly from major multi-million dollar endowments, the allocation of billions of dollars for sponsored research projects, and the numerous medical centers and facilities throughout the region. Furthermore, the University of Southern California's expansion project throughout the immediate vicinity to provide more student housing, more dorms, more class buildings, more research facilities, more parking structures, and more restaurants has resulted in the expedited gentrification process throughout the neighborhood. The urban revitalization plan was put forth by the Community Redevelopment Agency with the power of eminent domain to extort properties from local owners to sell the land to the University of Southern California board-of-directors. The result was a gentrification wave that left long-time residents priced-out of their homes and rent control reversals, which non-profit organizations within the community have since tried combating.

Another example lies within the Westside regional bloc of the City of Los Angeles, where a local unincorporated community has been abandoned by Culver City officials, and has been annexed by the City of Los Angeles. Located within the Westside regional bloc of the City of Los Angeles, the Mar Vista Gardens Housing Project is home to mostly low-income residents and recent immigrants from Mexico.

Although the housing project has a Culver City mailing address, like the Department of Motor Vehicles and the Pacific Division of the Los Angeles Police Department, its boundaries only border that of Culver City. Culver City officials view the Mar Vista Gardens area as an undesirable unincorporated community of the city of Los Angeles with no concrete plans to incorporate it into the city charter, yet no public officials have been bold enough to address or define the borders of the various communities.

The Mar Vista Gardens Housing Project is the westernmost, largest public housing project within the Housing Authority of the City of Los Angeles. However, the state-sponsored subsidized community is surrounded by wealthy neighbors and entertainment studio production companies. Westward are the unincorporated communities of Marina Del Rey, Playa Vista, and Playa Del Rey, some of the most affluent communities in the 11th District of the City of Los Angeles surrounded by the harbor and filled with million dollar homes.

Throughout the Mar Vista Housing Project, one of the most active street gang organizations within the Westside regional bloc has its headquarters. The Culver City 13 gang is technically based out of the City of Los Angeles, but adopted the name Culver City, and is as polarized as public officials about district boundaries.

In an attempt for district control, Culver City 13 gang members launched an urban struggle in the mid '90's against an African-American street gang, the Venice Shoreline Crips, who shared the projects with the Culver City 13 gang members. The racial urban warfare left numerous gang members on both sides incarcerated and murdered, which forced a gang injunction throughout the projects and Mar Vista in general so as to create a 'safety zone'. The street gang injunction led to harsh reductions in civil liberties, extreme curfews, and the expulsion of numerous gang members due to strict regulations.

Another unique example lies within the LAX Airport jurisdiction of the City of Los Angeles, but belongs to the county. It is the unincorporated community of Lennox, a community which is surrounded by one of the busiest and largest airports in the world, the aerospace industry, and private organizations such as Raytheon and Northrop. The community of Lennox serves as a cultural hub of the Westside regional bloc in that it appears to be one of the few areas within the jurisdiction that looks like it has been taken out of a Latin American developing country and has been strategically placed around beach city suburbs and LAX.

The citizens of the community of Lennox are mostly of Hispanic origin or recent immigrants, they have one of the lowest income levels per capita within the county, and many cannot speak English, which contributes to the low educational attainment level. The community has a high crime rate with delayed police response and involvement; consequently, the citizens do not get to vote on city measures nor city ordinances which affect their day to day lives. There is also high rate of teenage pregnancy and a lack of affordable housing, which is a widespread problem throughout the entire Los Angeles County.

A simple drive through the focal street within the community would make you believe you were driving through Tijuana, Mexico because many streets are impacted with liquor stores, taco stands, barber shops, butcher shops, small grocery stores, bakeries, strip clubs, prostitution, and street vendors selling: ice cream, corn on the cob, tacos, tamales, fruit, hot dogs, and pork rinds. Appropriately, the community has been nicknamed "Little Tijuana" by local and adjacent residents because of its close resemblance to the goods and services provided in Tijuana, Mexico.

The architecture used to build some of the elementary schools resembles California state prisons; fences are replaced with iron bars, the school colors are of a dull, grayish hue, few visible street signs identify a school crossing, and there are no speed bumps to reduce the speed of traffic within school zones. It is a poverty-stricken community with a high density level that renders serious traffic during school hours where narrow streets make it impractical to pick up children. Some schools, in fact, are located adjacent to adult video stores, strip clubs, and visible prostitution.

Many of the residents in the unincorporated community of Lennox provide low-skilled labor to the LAX Airport and the surrounding affluent neighborhoods. Some of these jobs include: waste management, janitorial services, cooking facilities, fast food service, maids, housekeepers, babysitters, truck/delivery drivers, ramp agents, mechanics, and many other essential jobs which directly contribute to the economy of the nation, the state, and the county.

However, many of these citizens are sometimes discriminated against, and they are largely ignored by law enforcement because they have no political representation. The private institutions surrounding the community are not reflective of the citizenry. Its depressed wages do not seem to fit within the context of a first world nation with a vibrant economy in a prestigious region of the Los Angeles County.

This phenomenon or social dichotomy is directly related to the economic gap between the rich and poor, which sometimes causes social and economic depression, combined with an alienated anxiety.

Poverty-stricken, high density, and overpopulated immigrant communities are often synonymous with gang activity because it is a way to cope with the social conditions which are experienced within those jurisdictions. The escapism which street gang organizations provides usually extends to drug and alcohol abuse, promiscuity, violence, crime, extortion, drug dealing, urban terrorism, prison life, and recidivism.

Street gang culture is a way to deal with the social paradox of existing in a world where the "American Dream" seems impossible to young working-class, minority adolescents who cannot match up to their white counterparts, but have a value system different from their immigrant parents. This essay will examine the philosophical, social, and political concepts of the Sureño culture according to street gangs in the Los Angeles County, the unique phenomenon of the Beach/LAX Airport/Westside regional bloc, and more specifically some of the aspects of the unincorporated community of Lennox, which will serve as an archetype for other gangs in the Los Angeles County.

CHAPTER 1: THE SOCIAL CONTRACT

According to Thomas Hobbes, "The state of nature is anarchic; it is a constant state of war of all against all. Human beings are in constant conflict between desires and power because the need to pursue those desires and power conflicts with that of others." There is no guarantee that individuals will secure that which they will covet in the future, thus they pursue what they covet immediately, which means they must secure those desires and power at another's expense.

Law enforcement agencies and legislation are created to hinder those desires and potential abuse of power by the more skillfully cunning individuals; therefore, the war of all against all is sanctioned into policies and procedures which fall within their judicial regulations.

Yet, even with legitimate authority in the form of law enforcement, city councils, and judicial process, those living according to subterranean street culture are mostly ignored and victimized by the legal political spectrum. Most do not have political representation, thus they operate under a different set of rules and norms. Many of those citizens who are disenfranchised are living in an enhanced anarchic state because there is no respect for recognized legal authority; therefore, several citizens have succumbed to lawlessness in the form of a social contract.

In the concrete jungle of the urban metropolis where lawlessness flourishes, there is no such phenomenon as justice or injustice. Many citizens provide personal sanctuary for themselves and protect their families by buying guns, locking doors, fencing yards, putting bars on windows, installing surveillance cameras or motion lights, and having guard dogs. They are in a constant state of war because they are competing for scarce resources in the form of desires and power.

The war of all against all is to protect themselves from the fear of danger and violent death, or to pursue their desires and power even though it conflicts with that of others'. The disenfranchised youth including: hoodlums, thieves, criminals, and drug dealers are in this constant state of war, while living in an anarchic state of nature. It is from this state of nature that they come together to pursue their self-preservation in the form of a social contract because they fear the constant war of all against all.

In the study of sociology, a term used to describe the competition for scarce resources in the form of over consumption and proliferation of material possessions is called "Catching up with the Joneses." In urban working-class neighborhoods there is no escaping this same phenomenon, specifically neighborhoods in close proximity of affluence. Many children of working-class parents see the affluence as an exit from poverty-stricken communities, as a way out of the miserable anxiety suffered in the urban metropolis.

Furthermore, different mediums of communication nourish the subconscious by conveying messages of trite expressions to try to progress in society through the social ladder, all of which maintain that at that exact moment in the child's life; the child has not developed his faculties. Overwhelming advertisements influence us to believe that the more material items you possess, the more respectable your life will be. These subliminal messages inform us that there is always the need for a new consumer product, which leads to the consistent oversaturated reinforcement; without a surplus of paper currency, an individual is insignificant and powerless.

Many disenfranchised communities in the Los Angeles County are made up of working-class immigrants who champion financial stability and try to improve their socio-economic status by joining the rat race, maintaining a hard-work ethic, occasionally participating in the political process, paying property taxes, and buying a new vehicle. Large portions of the immigrant population come from rural towns in Mexico or Central America and have difficulty adjusting to an urban metropolis which helps develop a more global perspective, but simultaneously detaches them from their community.

Because of the influence of affluence, this group of people also adopts the ideology of the prevalent economic gap and begins to participate in the "Catching up with the Joneses" paradigm with the same competitive fervor as does the rest of the dominant population. Many see an opportunity through the constant flow of drugs, criminal activities such as burglary and battery, intimidation through extortion, and other unconventional methods they can capitalize on to improve their socio-economic status.

It is through those alternative methods of financing luxury or material possessions, increasing their reputations through fear and intimidation, and protecting themselves from outsiders while maintaining peace within community boundaries that a social contract is created.

When a social contract has been established through necessity, there are always three fundamental principles for legitimate creation and involvement. Those three fundamental principles include: peace, prosperity, and protection. Foremost, peace is necessary to eliminate hostilities or disagreements, and to establish civic order amongst its members. Secondly, it is necessary for a social contract to have prosperity so that citizens can flourish with material wealth and possessions, and pursue financial independence free from impediments. Lastly, protection is necessary from foreign invasion, intruders, domestic disputes, and any other social factors which can contribute to injury or harm. The main reason to join the social contract is to have self-preservation in an anarchic concrete jungle which is controlled by lawlessness.

The social contract puts together informal mutual covenants and agreements which the participants can adhere to in order to secure their peace, prosperity, and protection in the community. Those who do not join the social contract must continue living in constant fear of danger and violent death because the social contract provides peace, prosperity, and protection to only those who have succumbed to the mutual covenants and agreements.

The continuity of fear is extended to those citizens who do not join the social contract and continue living within the boundaries of that community because it does not provide security to those outside of the social contract. Therefore, those who have not joined become open targets in the form of urban terrorism exercised by street gang members who are protected by the social contract. The social contract is then ratified through social norms and customs, coincidentally making it traditional street gang culture.

The social contract becomes legitimized and recognized by the consent of its members, by increased law enforcement, by paranoid citizens, by politicians who claim to rid the city of its gang problem, and the media which reports their criminal activities through various mediums of communication. Furthermore, those who join the social contract lose their natural freedom of existence.

They must now succumb to traditional customs which are not natural, however, in giving up some of their personal sovereignty, they gain security, civic freedom within their community, and an unlimited right to self-determination within the confinements of the social contract. The social contract provides members with unlimited liberties which are absent of external impediments within the street gang, but because of the significant presence of actual law enforcement agencies, they conduct their day to day activities clandestinely.

The social contract creates a collective body of individuals who are willing to risk their lives to preserve it, to defend it, or to fight for its honor against any opposition and foreign invasion. The social contract also adopts regulations and a district boundary created by government agencies, and gives it a name usually adopted by the actual city or the unincorporated community.

The social contract adopts real estate principles and adheres to the unwritten law of the right of first occupancy. They do not use bundles of rights, grant deeds, or security agreements to hold legal title, yet they congregate in different locations throughout their district boundaries including dead ends, main avenues, small streets, parks, corner intersections, and alleys. They execute the right of first occupancy by assembling in certain locations which become their cornerstones for drug trade commerce, which those areas then become real property.

They do not occupy territory with legal authority, yet they claim and occupy territory with fierce conviction, thus becoming usurpers of power. It is through this fundamental usurpation of power through intimidation, which becomes the basic authority for the social contract.

Because the name of the social contract has absolute authority and sovereignty for its members, the name of the city, street, or community is usually chosen to represent its members which is then publicly displayed in the form of graffiti or vandalism to demonstrate their significance of intimidation. These specific locations where they assemble become focal points of interest for its actual members, foreign rivals, political officials, law enforcement agencies, and different mediums of communication.

Most members belonging to a street gang organization have an overwhelming respect for their sovereign state which transcends the ordinary citizen to the level of a patriotic nationalist. It becomes commonplace for gang members to tattoo their bodies with the name of their street gang organization or social contract across their bodies, thus demonstrating that their sovereign state has absolute authority over them.

The members of the social contract are not allowed to contradict its absolute authority, nor are individual members allowed to maintain conflicting points of view with the original agreements of the social contract. Therefore, any behavior such as renouncing membership, switching allegiance, or not defending its honor results in denouncement or consequences.

Because the social contract is meant to maximize utility and provide the greatest good for the greatest amount of people, private interests become secondary because they are sometimes conflicting. The social contract is meant to secure group strength and power, it is supposed to make rights invincible, and it is supposed to make war upon hostile territories, instead of allowing its members to remain in an uncertain or precarious situation.

A flummoxing paradox exists with this phenomenon because the joining members gain peace within the street gang organization, prosperity pursuits within the community, and protection within their district boundary, but they now become vulnerable to the enemies of the sovereign state that did not exist before.

By membership proliferation, the social contract can inadvertently make war upon hostile territories because of stronger economic interests. Moreover, signs of good governance of the sovereign state can be witnessed when its membership voluntarily increases, yet some sovereign states coerce its citizens, oblige covenants, and impose a certain type of belief system. The latter becomes somewhat of an imperialist sovereignty which establishes colonies in other territories and implements administration over great distances because of its increased numbers.

In the Los Angeles County, the 18th St gang is one of the most expansive sovereign states as it has established colonies throughout different territories that were not within its original boundaries, yet it is one of the least cohesive organizations. There are significant disagreements within its competitive leadership, and they are one of the most loathed sovereignties within the Los Angeles County.

This type of imperialist observation is an interesting phenomenon because it demonstrates that residency in a specific boundary does not automatically indicate consent to that sovereign state. Because certain individuals do not acknowledge a sovereign state's authority and choose to join a different social contract, they become foreigners in their residential territory.

Moreover, on rare occasions siblings join opposing social contracts which leads to extreme adversarial consequences, thus they become complete enemies on the streets. However, there is no general contributing factor to this phenomenon and it must be assessed on a case-by-case basis.

The same is true for sovereign states which refuse the annexation of a larger street gang organization, and resist the colonization process of its members in order to remain autonomous. Some smaller sovereign states which lie within the boundaries of a larger street gang organization fluctuate between creating peace and making war with the larger street gang organization depending on diplomatic relationships they have established in the past, or enemies they have in common.

Sometimes, smaller gangs choose to separate from the larger sovereign states in order to resist domination and have the right to self-determination. Although many of those separatists might know most of the members of the larger street gang organization because they were matriculated at the same elementary or junior high schools and once even friends, at some point the leadership of the small sovereign states could decide that their liberties were being undermined by the larger street gang organization.

This phenomenon usually produces a new social contract with a new leadership, which results in aggression, hostility, denouncement, and expulsion from basic traditional boundaries. The new street gang organization usually annexes a small territorial radius, and the basic freedom to pursue their interests.

This significant demarcation usually results in street warfare between two sovereign states which exist within the same community, or share an intimate border. On the other hand, some smaller sovereign states become co-opted into the larger street gang organization out of necessity, out of common enemy interests, out of fear, or out of friendly relations.

Despite significant hostilities, gang member murders, and constant street warfare, those who have joined the social contract are not real or natural enemies. They are only enemies because of circumstance and situational relations, thus they are participating in street warfare for the sake of the social contract's authority.

As mentioned earlier, many of those gang members had friendly relations before joining the social contract, yet once involved they adopt the belief system which imposes a state of war amongst them. This means they are only accidental enemies and the state of war between them does not actually exist, it is a war of sovereign states and those gang members become soldiers or defenders of its honor.

Street warfare becomes a cyclical process which continues because the objective is to see the destruction of another sovereign state. Specifically if one protects the sovereign state with weapons, because the social contract establishes a state of war against hostile territories and gives its members absolute authority to destroy. If a gang member renounces his membership in a social contract, if he refuses or no longer wishes to defend the honor of that sovereign state, or if he puts down his weapons used to defend the sovereign state, he ceases to be an enemy and should no longer be a target of hatred or aggression.

Those who decide to renounce their membership in a social contract return to a civilian lifestyle and should be respected by adversaries because the right to kill them no longer exists. Those individuals should be allowed to pursue a life free from impediments such as street warfare, hostility and aggression, or disciplinary action.

CHAPTER 2: SECRET CRIMINAL SOCIETIES

All street gangs have established their sovereign social contract as a secret criminal society. Most secret societies throughout world history possess undisclosed information whether technological, political, economic, religious, operational, or metaphysical, and use it to their exclusive benefit. Street gangs possess subterranean economic and operational intelligence which is not available to all members of mainstream society. Therefore, they possess a valuable scarce commodity which is only available through exclusive membership.

Secret societies in Medieval Europe and Arabia were once formed on subversive platforms and worked against established authorities to pursue their objectives and desires, while others were formed in order to fight oppression or to resist tyrannical domination. Therefore, street gangs that have worked cooperatively for the protection of their communities or have fought oppression and domination against mainstream society can be said to have formed a secret criminal society based on subversive platforms.

By resisting the status-quo and oppression, they inadvertently form secret criminal societies sanctioned through a social contract which protects their general-law community, and thus become subversive units which operate throughout the Los Angeles County.

Many people who come from a low-level economic status feel goalless and powerless; therefore joining an organization which has some sort of goal or power can allow the individual to adopt power and goals that are not his own. When some of those goals and power are reached, the individual identifies with this process of attainment, which can be exploited by any such organization.

The ability of these organizations to proliferate quickly is due to their very nature of secrecy and mysticism, in order to maintain power. This invokes curiosity and confusion in most people; hence, the street gang becomes an antisocial organization which echoes fear and intimidation, thereby increasing membership amongst impressionable adolescents.

In forming secret criminal societies, gang members create an organizational culture which establishes norms, behaviors, customs, dress codes, and mannerisms. Dress codes are quite common in secret societies, such as The Assassins who wore white robes and red boots, or the witchcraft cults who wore black cloaks. Street gangs have also adopted their own dress code.

The dress code symbolizes uniformity and equality, which helps to reflect a battle dress posture amongst the members unless they have grand masters or high priests who might wear a more symbolic outfit with different colors which is usually obtained through seniority and leadership skills.

Amongst street gangs, veteran members who have become interested in fiscal policy, administration, and policy implementation are considered the high priests or grand masters because of their seniority, their work in the prison congress, or their leadership skills. Many of that leadership succumb to less conspicuous clothing so as to not invoke suspicion by law enforcement authorities.

Most street gang members come from low-income working-class families. As a result, many shop at local swap meets or military surplus stores where budgeting principles remain triumphant. This, in-turn, offers street gang members the convenience of purchasing a uniform which reflects gang attire while offering the benefits of being able to buy such garb within close proximity and affordability to their respective turfs.

For example, traditional gang attire often includes: inexpensive sneakers such as Converse (Chuck Taylor), Nike (Cortez), and Vans (late 70's slip-on) styles. House slippers commonly referred to as 'zigzags' or 'boulevards' also represent a further extension of footwear. This style of footwear is often worn with long white tube socks and oversized shorts, or oversized khakis and jeans.

The popular name brands are working-class such as Ben Davis, Dickies, Carlhart, or Levi's, which are oversized and commonly referred to as 'baggy' within the social norm. Traditional belts include a letter buckle usually with the beginning letter of the street gang organization or the nickname adopted by each specific gang member.

Also, oversized plain white t-shirts, polo shirts, button-downed Pendleton's, hooded or v-neck sweatshirts, plain black jackets, and sports jerseys. Dark-colored baseball caps, gloves commonly referred to as 'brownies', skullcaps, thick mustaches and beards, little facial hair, short hair or a bald head are all customs adopted by street gang members.

Throughout the greater Los Angeles County, many street gang members wear Los Angeles Dodgers or Oakland Raiders sports gear as a symbol of patriotism. They do so because such dark, solid colors reflect a strong message of aggression and patriotism towards the common masses. Coincidentally, street gangs and sports clubs often exist within a constant competitive state of warring nature, albeit the latter are performed through publicly sanctioned sporting events.

Ultimately, such dress code symbolizes the resistance of the status-quo, the overt display of membership to foreign intruders, observers, or officials of law enforcement agencies. This is done in order to produce fear and intimidation by publicly displaying the dress code of those who participate in urban warfare within the concrete jungle.

Secret societies often speak in code, use signs and symbols, develop handshakes, and inflict self-mutilation which also becomes part of the custom and norm. Some secret societies in Europe were trained in languages to disguise clandestine activities or objectives; similarly, most street gang members speak in code as they have developed a simple, yet unconventional dialect which includes back-slang that is not easily understood by the general population.

In prison, many of these gang members learn and speak indigenous languages to continue clandestine operations as a form of secrecy. They also use sign language for communication or to spell out their neighborhoods, or adopt a letter or combination of letters to identify their gang which becomes recognizable to enemies and observers.

Handshakes are commonly used, usually with a clever sequence of shakes with the shake usually ending with their main gang sign, which is also traditional in other secret societies. Because of their strange and abnormal customs, their utter lack of respect for law enforcement, their undesirable and terrorizing activities, and their subversive nature, their inscrutable reputation leaves the community stunned into dismay.

Many secret societies use numerology as part of their custom. Street gangs also use traditional numerological symbols to identify street gang culture. Most of the Southern Californian, Mexican-American gangs use the number 13 after their neighborhood in graffiti-style pictographs because it represents the 13th letter of the alphabet which is also the letter M for Mexican.

However, most Mexican-American gangs in Northern California use the number 14 after their neighborhood to represent the 14th letter in the alphabet, which also stands for Northerners or Norteños. In the case of African-American street gangs, their neighborhood will most always be followed by a bloods or crips, which they also represent with colored clothing articles and bandanas for identification purposes; blue for crips, red for bloods.

The origins of the colored handkerchief phenomenon began in the 1950's with prison authorities in California who distributed blue/red railroad handkerchiefs to the different factions for work purposes within the Mexican-American demographic. The Southern Californian Mexican-Americans opted for the blue handkerchiefs, while the Northern Californian Mexican-Americans chose the red handkerchiefs.

Thus, for the Mexican-American gangs, the colored bandanas are more prevalent as a prison division, rather than a street division like the African-American street gangs. Therefore, Mexican-American gangs from Southern California have become known as Southernists or Sureños, and in Northern California they are Northerners or Norteños.

Additionally, weaponry and religious figures which symbolize how they live by the sword and spirit, like the Knights Templar, are cherished gang symbols. Most Mexican-American gang members have Catholic leanings because the majority of Hispanics are of Catholic descent, thus the 'sword and spirit' duality exists within their social contract similar to other secret societies.

As the name suggests, the Castrators of Russia used self-mutilation as a way of achieving mystical insight. Tribal societies in New Zealand and Australia used tattooing, markings, and piercings to reach a state of excitement, ritual, or a symbol of hierarchical structure. These methods of self-mutilation became a cultural norm for members of secret societies which had to endure a high tolerance for pain to demonstrate their courage and fearlessness.

Street gangs use similar self-mutilation methods to maintain rituals and norms that become part of the organizational culture such as tattooing, markings, and piercings. Common tattoos amongst Mexican-

American gang members in the Los Angeles County include: three dots in the form of a triangle to represent 'my crazy life', the Los Angeles Dodgers emblem to symbolize patriotism, a Mongolian warrior/jinni or Aztec warriors which symbolize courage and background, Aztec/Mayan calendars and pyramids which represent ethnic heritage, and old English letters to represent their neighborhood, their last name, their clique or their regional bloc.

For Southernists, the number 13 is usually incorporated after the neighborhood in handwriting, old English, or block letters. Song dedications usually from old school love songs often called 'oldies' such as 'Smile Now Cry Later' called a chain, which is normally a chain-like tattoo around the neck, and other such symbols that have become representative of the lifestyle including: jokers, clowns, Lowrider vehicles, prison bars, fearsome-looking mascots, devils, and girls with spaghetti-looking hair.

Also common in Southernist gangs are portraits of the Virgin Mary, Jesus Christ, praying hands with a rosary around them, or crosses which suggest a strong Catholic background, although devils and clowns could exist in the same collage usually exhorting duality. Although pierced ears, tongues, lips, and eyebrows are common, more emphasis is placed on the symbolic tattooing to maintain the status-quo amongst the participating members.

Furthermore, those with the most, the largest, or the most noticeable tattoos are usually looked upon as the most courageous and fearless within the street gang organization.

Some ancient secret societies maintained religious objectives or included religious-magical rituals to attain a state of excitement. Several use a combination of Catholic religion, paganism, and primitive superstition to incorporate the ideology into their symbolic tattooing and thought process in general. Two of the most notorious gangs in the Downtown/ Central Los Angeles regional bloc are MS (Mara Salva Trucha) and 18th St., which are rumored to be satanic devil worshippers who revere wickedness, who terrorize and murder victims with absolute brutality, and who sometimes are compared to sinister cults that practice black magic or sacrifice.

Many of the gang members come from civil war-torn countries in Central America including: El Salvador, Nicaragua, and Honduras, many of whom have witnessed dead and decayed bodies in public streets, many have witnessed heartless executions, and many have been desensitized to consistent brutality.

Several of these individuals were displaced from their countries for political reasons and arrived in the United States as political refugees seeking asylum, but were unaware of a different type of street warfare that existed in the urban metropolis of the Los Angeles County. Different types of pressure-groups exist wherever humanity congregates in any part of the world, thus many of those political refugees became absorbed by the social contract in order to maintain their survival and have protection in their community.

Numerous political refugees who joined the street gangs were absorbed by the criminal ideology, thus further contributing to the high rate of Hispanic inmates throughout the state of California. In turn, overcrowded state prisons and local jails, which became overwhelmed with inmates, forced federal government agencies to ratify eradication policies to facilitate the dense prison population.

Therefore, federal agencies took necessary steps to deport illegal immigrants who were arrested for gang/criminal activity and sent them back to Central America or Mexico. This deportation of illegal criminal immigrants has caused a nationwide panic in a few Central American countries because of their sinister nature, because of their rapid expansion, and because of the importation of Los Angeles-based street culture within their borders. (See Ch 10.)

Most secret societies adopt rituals which include: initiation rites, exclusive membership, and fiduciary agreements or obligations. In common secret societies, oath taking, vows of silence or secrecy, adopting principals, and imposing exclusive membership promote myth and ritual with special meaning to its participants designating organizational norms.

In street gangs, the initiation rites usually include a physical beating, the adoption of a pseudonym, the choosing of a clique or partisanship, and in some cases a criminal act of violence to demonstrate loyalty or fearlessness. Under exclusive membership, many street gang members have a probationary period to demonstrate loyalty and courage, sometimes they are examined prior to initiation rites, some have a makeshift trainee program where an individual actually participates in clandestine activities without going through the initiation rites, and many are tested randomly for loyalty and courage.

Fiduciary agreements and obligations include: upholding the social contract and defending its honor regardless of whoever denounces it, not retreating in battle regardless of the odds, demonstrating fearlessness or barbaric ruthlessness, embracing all ages of potential recruits, not leaving the organization after the initiation process, and enforcing a strict policy of non-betrayal against a fellow member. Defecting from the street gang organization, retrieving in defeat, not upholding the social contract, and showing fear can lead to severe penalties or repercussions, however, betraying a fellow member usually results in their own type of jurisprudence, which usually involves execution.

Several secret societies develop certain behaviors or mannerisms which can be considered tasteless or harmful such as: debauchery, induced drug use, and alcohol consumption to produce ecstasy and enhanced mental states. Many street gang members are known for their excesses of debauchery, fornication with promiscuous women, and indiscriminate sexual relations.

Orgiastic drumming was common in some tribal secret societies, which can sometimes be witnessed in modern street gangs at local parties or gatherings which would include 'freaking', which are stimulating dances which involve vulgar sexual perversion, or promiscuous behavior which produces 'player-status.' Although debauchery and drug or alcohol use is not necessarily expected nor imposed, it is heavily encouraged in pressure groups and even becomes ritual for some members. However, it could also be viewed as an excuse for licentiousness.

Because these pressure groups are consistently engaged in street warfare and criminal activities, the need to experiment or induce laborious violence through drug/alcohol abuse is quite normal, which in turn becomes customary. It is common for young, vulnerable adolescents to try to impress the grand masters or high priests, their subordinates, and their peers.

Therefore, many gang members rely on alcohol or drug use for ecstasy that is produced by excitatory methods followed by manipulation of the mind. Some of these participants use drugs to produce enhanced mental states, while many use them for simple recreational purposes, for ritual purposes, or to simply escape from reality, thus leading to drug addiction. Fear and intimidation are such significant factors in pressure groups, because one single criminal activity can cost the member his life.

For example, going to prison or getting killed on behalf of the gang are common consequences. The philosophy of the street gang organization is that one man or group of men can have absolute power over another's decision-making authority, thus resulting in the absolute authority of the social contract.

Adopting surnames is common in secret societies because of its very nature of secrecy, the ease of identification amongst themselves, decipherable hieroglyphics on surfaces which only some can recognize, and a personification of something outside of themselves. For example, some street gang members adopt animal names to personify an animal because of their characteristic which cannot be done by any common man or because of their resemblance to the animal.

Some of these names include: Grizzly, Cricket, or Termite. Other names are adopted because of the way the individuals look such as: Sporty, Baby-Face, or Shady. Various names are adopted because of the reverence for evil such as: Wicked, Diablo, or Spooky. Descriptive names are adopted because the individuals behave a certain way such as: Wacky, Rascal, or Boxer. Select names are taken from cartoon characters such as: Boo-Boo, Scrappy, Dopey, or Spanky.

And still others are taken from 'oldies music' such as: Puppet, Lil' Boy, Stranger, or Shy-Boy. After many popular names have been exhausted they start to become innovative to avoid the recycling of names, but the actual process itself has become an organizational norm.

Street gang organizations engage in fraternal behavior which is also linked to liberty and equality. By developing a fraternity masked behind a secret society and social contract, the experiences that are shared bonds the members rather closely. The rituals, norms, mannerisms, and behaviors are so commonplace that when they are altered, the entire group becomes disillusioned.

They have succumbed to the organizational culture also called 'groupthink.' Sharing experiences that include: drug/alcohol rituals, scars from the battle zone, events and scenes from the historical street warfare, close encounters of death and violence, time spent in prison, criminal activities, nights of debauchery and sexual perversion, paying homage to friends who have been murdered, and other such factors that bond people together allows for the fraternal state of mind that has developed amongst them. Over the years, they become nostalgic and talk about the organizational culture and recall how they were able to survive through cooperation in urban warfare.

Street gangs are community-oriented as they have stressed the community over the individual. Ironically, they terrorize the community by usurping territory, by gaining recruits and converts by appealing to sensationalism, by glorifying violence, and by dedicating themselves to fraternity, money, and power. The fraternal behavior helps to develop a sense of equality with individuality because the objective is the same; to defend the community, while the liberty is expressed with the licentiousness and ability to pursue criminal activities without impediments.

Arkon Daraul maintains that, "The uniqueness of the true secret society is that certain aspects of human thought which are particularly compelling are combined to train and maintain the efforts of a group of people to operate in a certain direction."

The true objective of the secret society is to develop a collective body of individuals who subject themselves voluntarily to an organizational culture that has absolute sovereignty over their decision-making authority. Secret societies around the world have similar objectives including: the desire for power, love of mystery, sense of being someone special, sense of belonging, and the feeling that one will gain something extraordinary by membership. Any organization that can accommodate that phenomenon on a large scale can exploit a certain demographic and population for a means of attaining power.

Some law enforcement authorities and several non-participants of urban warfare believe that because street gang members only persecute each other, they should be left to their own devices. However, this type of detached thinking changed when innocent murder victims increased significantly and criminal activities started becoming more rampant. As they become larger in size and membership proliferates, the need to develop a more central authority and to separate into factions as cliques becomes necessary. The next chapter will examine cliques as political parties and how partisanship becomes a significant role in policy implementation or public administration.

CHAPTER 3: POLITICAL PARTIES

In order to have central authority and carry out administrative efforts, a hierarchical structure is needed to maintain stability. Those that make up the central authority in a hierarchical structure exercise some type of authority to try to carry out policies; however, their opinions or paradigms can cause a conflict of interest. Because the difference in opinions causes division, factions develop and the centralized governance becomes polarized. Political parties have developed throughout history because of this phenomenon and the governance of a street gang organization which has become a general-law community with central authority is no exception.

As street gangs increase, they begin to develop cliques which soon begin to adopt certain names and ideologies that become representative of that group of individuals. When young adolescents begin the initiation process and start to adopt the rituals, customs, and behaviors of a street gang organization, they sometimes choose partisanship and decide which clique they identify with and register themselves with that particular party.

The larger the street gang organization, the more cliques/parties emerge, however, there are several smaller gangs which do not have any parties and are highly centralized, while others only have a two-party system. In 'State and Local Government,' Bowman and Kearney maintain that, "Parties function as umbrella organizations that shelter loose coalitions of relatively like-minded individuals."

This is true for street gangs as well because their different cliques are the umbrella organizations which shelter like-minded individuals who create or join certain parties based on identification, geography, or social-economic status. Some parties are created because of straight partisan differences; some are created around the age of its members, some because of geographical location, and some because of social class differences.

Party identification is sometimes created before an individual registers with that party, after they have joined the street gang organization, and sometimes members switch allegiance because their interests are not parallel with that of the parties, or because their interests have shifted to another party.

The ideological spectrum recognizes five ideologies as the most common. Most political parties around the world are loosely created around these broad ideas. Looking at the ideological spectrum from left to right, each ideology will be shortly summarized and identified as follows:

Radical—at the left of the spectrum considered leftists, willing to overthrow central authority through violence or revolution, large government involvement, and using extreme methods for change.

Liberal—Government should promote the social welfare of the population, want gradual change within the current system and status quo, and reject hostile takeover of government.

Moderate—Share views with most parties, tolerant of others' views and do not have extreme views of their own, and stand with different groups from issue to issue.

Conservative—Traditional views and maintaining the status quo, cautious about adopting new policies especially if significant change will take place, and less government involvement.

Reactionary—At the end of the spectrum considered the extreme right, want to go back to the good old days, and use repressive force to achieve goals.

Many gangs follow the spectrum inadvertently and create factions which represent the different positions or issues. When an impressionable individual decides to join the social contract, he is subconsciously making a decision to join a clique based on social and economic issues while considering such factors as government changeability, flexibility, government involvement, and repression.

When joining a smaller street gang organization that does not have party identification because it does not exist, such factors are not considered and membership is strictly based on the absolute authority of that sovereign state. Street gangs which have political parties hold their party and sovereign state as a dual governing authority, however, it is sometimes mixed and sometimes identification is stronger with the party rather than the sovereign state, or vice versa.

The Lennox 13 street gang organization will be assessed in this section including the identification of its divided cliques as political parties and as a multiparty system showing how they fit into the ideological spectrum. There are more political parties within the Lennox 13 street gang organization, yet those below resemble the ideological spectrum much closer and will be considered major parties, while those not represented will be considered minor parties. Many Southernists throughout the Los Angeles County maintain the same names for their different cliques; therefore, the Lennox 13 example is one which could be mirrored in other street gang organizations.

Jokers—on the far left of the spectrum, considered subversives and unconventional, willing to overthrow existing authority and go against the status quo, use violence and revolution to implement change.

Night-Owls—central government should promote welfare of all of the members, gradual change is desirable, and do not want violent takeover of central authority.

Peewee Locos—side with those on the right and left on certain issues, tolerate views of all cliques and no extreme views of their own.

Tokers—traditional views of street life culture and maintain status quo, skeptical of new policies that will introduce unconventional ideas, and less government involvement.

Winos—at the end of the spectrum considered the far right, want to use repressive force to produce change, and want to take the neighborhood back to the good old days.

Each political party within the Lennox 13 street gang organization has a central committee which is the decision-making body for the clique. The committee then selects nominees to represent their political party within the central authority by caucus or informal small meetings. Once a representative is chosen, he will serve as the liaison between the political party and the central authority. The representative usually has good diplomacy skills, good communication skills, he is well-liked, and he has demonstrated good leadership skills.

The central committee is self-appointed and the nominees are not chosen by the constituency or the rest of the clique, yet they are hand-picked by committee incumbents, which is an elitist unit that usually has a party agenda and seems to be well organized and revered by its constituency.

Often times the representative chosen will be from the central committee. The street constituency is considered the rest of the members of the political party who do not have what C. Jillson considers, "Requisite experience, stability, and judgment, to play a full role in the political life of the community."

Only those who belong to the committee have collective decision-making authority and their power is exercised through acquiescence, however, there is room for climbing up the social ladder from the constituent level through demonstration of courageous efforts and close relationships with those in the committee.

Those in the committee can benefit from the spoils of politics including: access to public funds, high-level political offices, government contracts including assassinations, and other various opportunities. Similar to other government bodies, they are not above corruption, scandals, or patronage.

The political parties in the Lennox 13 street gang organization also have a headquarters where they hold formal/informal meetings, caucuses, secret criminal society rituals, capital-intensive programs, and other miscellaneous activities. When the central committees choose a representative and send him off as an appointed official serving as a liaison between the political party and central authority, he represents his district, which is also the headquarters.

Although the headquarters is mostly party-oriented, individuals from other parties/cliques are welcome and many times encouraged to travel through as transients or permanents to others' headquarters. It is not rare when members from other political parties spend a great amount of their time at a different headquarters establishing diplomatic relations, or simply having a better sense of fraternity with members of another party, which does not mean they are not loyal to their own party.

On the contrary, those political parties who host the diplomat use this factor to enhance public opinion throughout the street gang organization, and the diplomat gets a better sense of belonging because their loyalty transcends party-lines.

However, this is not to say that there is not weak partisanship; sometimes self-destructive behavior, weak partisanship, and dubious loyalty results in physical discipline at the constituency level because most political parties are image-oriented. Self-destructive behavior in the form of drug abuse is ridiculed or frowned upon. Weak partisanship shows a weak party apparatus, and dubious loyalty can be considered cynical, hence, physical discipline or verbal reprimands are implemented because image and respect is top priority.

Diplomats can sometimes sit at a central committee hearing of another party, yet they cannot vote on policy issues or other decisions which require a three-fourths majority. Despite political parties' headquarters and party loyalty, conventions are held on a regular basis on main focal points of any street gang organization. At these locations they represent and uphold the social contract where all members interact, discuss, and lobby. They also host other street gangs with entertainment such as festivals and sports activities, which will be looked at further in Chapter 12.

These political party structures do not run a democratic process because they do not use primaries, elections, initiatives, referendums, campaigns, or the civil service system to put their party in the majority, however, they are motivated to work together and try to obtain or remain in power. Moreover, they do use the recall to remove certain members from office either through convention where the citizenry is allowed to express their opinions, or by physical force.

For example, in 1995, the Lennox 13 street gang had a representative (Chino from the Winos) of the conservative right who was part of the central committee, and who had served long and numerous prison terms. He was big in stature, used repressive force amongst fellow gang members, and continuously subjugated subordinates to ridicule, taxation without representation, discipline, or forced labor. He would also hold council meetings at his party's headquarters to accuse other party members of extreme partisanship, sectarianism, dissent, or government polarization.

The city council structure had tried neutralizing his coercive behavior while encouraging him and those in his party to use diplomatic means to interact with fellow gang members. Most of his constituency and party-members distanced themselves from him because they did not support his repressive behavior, yet they feared him because of his reputation, his size, and his career.

The city council held a private meeting and decided that a recall was necessary to remove him from office, thus they leaked the information to the underground media and held a caucus at a neutral convention center, which was the Lennox Middle School. At the caucus, his repressive behavior had been documented and released for public scrutiny, and now he was being held accountable for his actions thereby subjecting him to discipline and recall.

His discipline was brutal and bloody, which left him hospitalized with broken bones. He was completely removed from public office; he then withdrew himself from the street gang organization all together.

The goal of the political party structure is to place some of its members at the central authority level, which has executive decision-making control and which is responsible for implementing and interpreting legislative policies they can draft up or benefit from. Some of those policies will require multiparty consensus, thus political parties compete to present alternative programs to the overall population on how to maintain security, opportunity, and progress.

During conventions or appointments of political figures, the central committees which represent their constituency choose candidates that range from radical to reactionary on the ideological spectrum to represent the attitudes of their party and reflect the public mood. Political parties are a great way to maintain stability and competition for power because of a polarized and decentralized street gang organization; however factions can lead to extreme opposition and dissent, unhealthy divisions within the public, difficult public administration, dubious public interest, and sometimes civil war.

CHAPTER 4: CITY COUNCIL STRUCTURE

After a street gang organization has adopted a social contract, after it has established itself as a secret society-type organization, and after it has divided itself between competing factions, it must create stability and order through a governing structure to provide overall leadership. The members of the governing structure, also called "shot-callers," must create a system that becomes their standard of operations and defines procedures in order to have somewhat of a functioning government. They do not have a charter or written constitution to outline their local government structure or their objectives, yet they do adopt some basic structures of a typical city council similar a general-law city.

As political parties/cliques congregate at their headquarters and discuss the day-to-day issues amongst their party members, social concerns which affect the well-being of the citizenry must be addressed and communicated to higher levels of authority. The parties' central committees handle issues which affect party members and make decisions based on the well-being of their constituency; however, the central authority is responsible for discussing/debating issues and passing policies which affect the overall well-being of the entire street gang organization.

Those who make up the central authority are the city council members and are chosen from the competing factions. Many adopt elitist theory behavior and believe they naturally possess leadership skills or can make better informed decisions, most serve on the central committees of their parties, and most have served prison terms, which amongst the citizenry yields respect, admiration, fear, and intimidation. Because fear and intimidation are such important factors in exercising power and authority, those gang members who possess extraordinary courage, barbaric ruthlessness, seniority, and charismatic leadership skills, will eventually be considered for decision-making authority, or will assume leadership through self-appointment.

In most street gangs, self-appointment is approved amongst peers and subordinates after the gang member has returned from active duty in prison (see Chapter 7) and underground news articles have been circulating through word-of-mouth about the individual's extraordinary accomplishments or efforts. This type of publicity is beneficial to the individual's reputation because when he returns from a prison term, his authority is usually tacit and needs no consent. He warrants unlimited respect, which is another important factor in gang culture, and he can impose policies that are immediately enforced.

At the highest level of governance in a city council structure is the mayor, which has overall leadership, and executes policies for the entire community. A street gang organization has the same position without the official title and is usually considered the major shot-caller. Moreover, in actual political organizations the label is given to the person who occupies the position, but in a street gang organization it is the surname itself which renders the respect and admiration because an individual's name and reputation can carry a lot of weight.

This is sometimes an elected official or a self-appointed position depending mostly on circumstance rather than structure. He is usually chosen from the city council, moves into the position immediately after serving a prison term, and has the luxury of chairing any meeting of any political party. City councils usually have four types of structures which include:

Mayor-council (Strong mayor with lots of executive authority and limited authority to city council.)

Weak-Mayor council (Which limits mayor role to figurehead, host, or greeter, and serves ceremonial tasks such as public speaking and chairing meetings.)

Council-Manager (Strong city council that makes and executes policy.)

City-commission form (In which commissioners make policy as members of the city's governing board.)

Amongst street gang organizations, the city commissioner is the most popular form of government because the city council members can be both policymakers and policy executors serving as administrators and legislators. Usually, one commissioner is designated as figurehead to preside over the city council meetings. They do not have enough members, revenues, and expertise to run an actual staff which separates administrative from legislative duties, thus the city commission form works best.

In several street gangs, it is not rare to have a mayoral figurehead run his administration like a dictatorship or a mixed government to enforce policies through coercion or repression. Often, the self-appointed dictator will serve a term in prison and return with Machiavellian intentions to execute policies through fear and intimidation, and then deceive the citizenry through lies or deception.

A dictator often has a small government and imposes high taxes so that those in the commission can benefit from a large share of the city's budget or allocated resources for themselves. The city council members will usually acquiesce to the policies of the mayor/dictator if they benefit from the spoils of politics, if not, serious divisions in government can result in succession and even civil war.

The city council members have a duty to their constituency and to their political party if they represent a clique, and must pass or veto policies with their constituency in mind. The city councils usually hold weekly or monthly council meetings where they discuss and compromise issues in regards to policy, budget, and maintenance. There is usually an agenda and most record the minutes of the day and go back to their constituency and/or political party to discuss issues in greater detail with their central committees or sometimes their entire constituency.

In general, citizens want to be well-governed and feel like they have some involvement in the political process. Therefore, the challenge to the city council is to provide goods and services such as weapons or drugs in a timely manner, they must remain receptive to structural improvements, there should be tranquility among public officials, and they should allow for change within the government allowing for flexibility.

Sometimes the city council becomes uneven because a district or political party might be underrepresented; therefore, a group of citizens can become disenfranchised resulting in factions, high turnover rate, or loss of membership.

A street gang organization can be easily managed because the council members and the constituency come from the same socioeconomic stratum, they share the same political philosophy, and they are always homogenized urban communities. Most city councils within street gangs succumb to the elitist leadership theory in which a small group of individuals or leaders exercise power and enjoy a strategic advantage in influencing government decisions. Because the mayor is the central authority figure, his ultimate task is to maintain the peace, prosperity, and protection amongst the citizenry and pass policies which reflect this philosophy.

CHAPTER 5: BUDGETING PRINCIPLES

In order to continue maintenance in any organization, the allocation of monies is necessary for its existence. The way a street gang is organized with its city council, political parties, and central authority; budgeting principles are required to maintain sovereignty and protection from hostile aggression. The government is responsible for delivering goods or services in a timely manner; therefore, it is the fiduciary duty of city council members and those with decision-making authority to provide those services so that the citizenry can uphold the social contract at all costs.

Street gang organizations are in a constant state of street warfare, therefore defense spending becomes the largest portion of its allocation of resources. Gangs adopt the principles of taxing, spending, and intergovernmental relations with the prison congress, which in turn contributes to the economic necessity of their organization. Financing any organization can be an arduous task, thus a street gang must introduce a budget cycle and examine its revenues and expenditures on a regular basis.

In the state of California, local governments rely on the state assembly for funding that has trickled down from the federal government. The federal government collects taxes from several sources, distributes monies to state governments, and the states distribute those monies to counties and local governments. This is considered 'intergovernmental relations' which government agencies and organizations rely on one another for resources. The same is true for street gangs; however, the prison congress is more dependent on gang members on the outside to provide economic assistance.

For obvious reasons, commerce and business is facilitated from the outside, therefore the prison congress collects taxes from the city councils on the outside, which becomes a good source of revenue for the prison congress. It is rare for a sovereign street gang organization on the outside to refute the tax imposed by the prison congress; however, it did happen during the 'Treaty of the South Side' with the tax revolt of the Maravilla gangs, which resulted in liquidation and catastrophe. (See Chapter 11)

Since most street gang organizations can collect from their own sources rather than the prison congress, the city councils are responsible for financing their own administrations. Whether the administration is liberal or conservative, taxing and spending principles revolve around commerce and defense spending because of the constant state of war. Most street gangs have a *laissez-faire* or hands-off economy with limited regulation. This basically means that individuals are allowed or encouraged to pursue business ventures, but can later be taxed at a higher level because of their ability to pay more, hence the regulation.

Most city councils levy a progressive income tax in which an increase in their contribution is directly influenced by the percentage of their income. City council members of a street gang organization promote entrepreneurship or business ideas in order to rely heavily on the personal income tax for revenues because it is the easiest to impose. Street gang administrations collect revenues from: individual, business or corporation, general sales, property, transportation, and other miscellaneous taxes. Individual taxes can be collected from any members of the constituency that have a legal or civilian job or from any gang member who is engaged in capital-intensive programs such as drug selling or stealing cars.

Business or corporate taxes can be collected from any member who has established an actual business such as a sole proprietorship, partnership, or corporation and can contribute a larger portion due to his ability-to-pay. General sales taxes are imposed on any such products which can be purchased on the black market such as drugs, guns, and ammunition, and can be purchased above cost. Property taxes are collected from city councils on the outside as a means to protect its fellow members in jail from hostile aggression and paid to the prison congress.

Inmates in jail and prison are considered real and movable property in the form of protection, and although it seems abstract, it is a good source of revenue for the prison congress. The transportation tax is imposed informally because instead of having a motor fuel or vehicle licensing fee, the city council mandates a contribution tax when a vehicle is commandeered for commerce, business, or war. The individual must surrender his vehicle for utilitarian purposes.

There are other miscellaneous taxes, for example; the Lennox 13 street gang organization engages in tourism, which means they rob tourists because of the proximity of the airport. However, miscellaneous taxes are usually regional or circumstantial.

After gangs have collected revenues and levied taxes on the citizenry using basic banking skills, they must spend those monies in areas where they can deliver more goods or services to the general public. The city councils impose a general income tax on political parties (if no political parties exist, individuals are taxed) and it is up to the central committee of the political party to collect those revenues from their constituency.

The personal income tax is then collected by the central committees and distributed to the city council which in turn gets placed in a general or special fund. Monies for guns, drugs, ammunition, the prison congress, and transportation go to the general fund, while monies for healthcare, funeral arrangements, and other miscellaneous items, which are also regional and circumstantial, go to the special fund.

Street gang organizations have expenditures which include: housing and community development, public safety, defense spending, parks and recreation, healthcare, transportation, and culture/leisure. Housing and community development expenditures include rent, lease, or mortgage payments to homes or motels which provide drug traffic and contribute directly to the gross domestic product (GDP).

Public safety expenditures include military defense spending on weapons, ammunition, and patrol units who observe the urban complex, like a neighborhood watch program, to keep surveillance of possible intruders or foreign invasion. Parks and recreation expenditures include contributions to any events held at a local park including sporting events, barbecues, conventions, and secret criminal society-type rituals.

Healthcare expenditures include contributions to hospitalized patients or their families, sometimes contributions to funeral expenses; however, the healthcare expenditures are arbitrary and subject to personal volunteerism.

There is no state-sponsored healthcare program, and the burden usually lies with the victim's family. There are transportation expenditures including maintenance, gas, mileage, stealing/stripping vehicles, and culture/leisure expenditures including musical festivals, sporting events, and typical conventions or gatherings. There are also miscellaneous expenditures including attorney fees or public contributions to incarcerated members, yet this is also an arbitrary expenditure and usually based on the rapport the inmate has with certain members of his constituency.

Within street gang organizations, the mayor proposes the budget to the city council based on projections and assessments, but they do not adhere to an actual fiscal year budget cycle. Street gangs do not have a department of finance; rather the budget is mostly dependent on the mayor's speculations. It is not a democratic process because taxing and spending procedures are not transparent, nor can public officials be held accountable because there is no way to prove if an administration is in a deficit, or if they have a surplus.

Street gangs do not use a line item budget, which allows council members to veto specific lines from the budget proposal, but they do categorize expenditures and revenues by function or character. It does require a majority approval by the city council, it does take into consideration debt incurred, and it is particular about preventing expenditures from exceeding revenues.

Although street gang organizations are affected by intergovernmental relations with the prison congress, most sovereign street gang organizations enjoy a substantial amount of autonomy. Moreover, when street gang organizations are financially constrained, they must find a way to increase taxes from their available sources. However, the funding must be spent on goods or services demanded by the public and it should reflect policies which benefit the welfare of the populous.

CHAPTER 6: TYPES OF POLICIES AND IMPLEMENTATION

The administrative structure of a complex organization is known as a bureaucracy, which is a nonpartisan profession in order to achieve public administration. Therefore, in street gang organizations, the bureaucracy is made up of the city council members who are responsible for legislative and administrative duties because they cannot separate both functions and must implement policies using nonpartisan discretion.

The city council members of a street gang usually represent a political party, therefore it is essential to public administration that when implementing policies which affect the overall community, they do so with nonpartisan intentions and adhere to a utilitarian philosophy. To be successful in conventional politics, a career politician must learn the art of compromise because the decision-making process is one of making choices through a process of conflict, bargaining, and accommodation.

In order for the bureaucracy to have a well-functioning process, policy implementation must be based on standards which are applicable to all individuals uniformly. Basically, well-made policies should affect all members of the street gang organization equally and the rules should also produce predictable and certain outcomes on a day-to-day basis without ambiguity. This is not an easy task because policies can often produce imprecise and contradictory goals, and they can be partial to certain groups of individuals.

As was noted in chapter 2, many Mexican-American street gang organizations revere evil, while simultaneously maintaining a strong catholic leaning. A basic policy which they implement is the separation of church and state. In order for the culture of a street gang organization to be free from religious worship, a secular society must be secured so that religious piety does not get in the way of street warfare. Rousseau wrote that, "Good Christians make bad citizens," which implies that a good Christian is only interested in serving the clergy and will make a bad citizen because he/she will not be interested in serving or obeying the sovereign state.

In street gangs, the state has absolute sovereignty, thus to die for one's sovereign state is patriotic and dutiful. If a member of the street gang organization is murdered while demonstrating extreme courage, he dies as a martyr and is remembered as serving the sovereignty of the state with duty and obligation, and was consumed by love of state and glory.

During street warfare many citizens are bloodthirsty and intolerant due to the organizational culture of a street gang, thus some members breathe murder and slaughter, which becomes a religious experience during the state of war. It is the duty of the city council to refrain from passing policies which interfere with the opinions of the citizens and how they deal with internal ethics and morality because they are constantly engaged in antisocial behavior and street warfare, thus they should not be burdened with a dual obligation with church and state that places them in contradiction with themselves.

It is the duty of the administration to remove those citizens from the social contract who choose not to adhere to the absolute authority of the sovereignty and refuse to sacrifice themselves to their obligation or civil duties. Individuals are constantly encouraged and tested for loyalty, bravery, and sacrifice to see if the street gang organization has absolute sovereignty over them and how much sovereignty individuals are willing to surrender.

According to organizational theory, a 'prisoner's dilemma' exists when there is a conflict of interest between two parties and both parties are trying to maximize their self-interest. The conflict exists when one party acts out of self-interest and their decision adversely affects the other party, therefore they are in a prisoner's dilemma because neither party knows the other's actions.

The best solution to the prisoner's dilemma is for both parties to remain quiet, avoid incriminating themselves and the other party, and walk away from the situation unscathed. This is the most significant policy implemented because the consistent criminal activity and street warfare necessitates the suppression of information.

There is an exception to this policy because some information is shared amongst policy makers, members of central committees, some constituents, and other fraternal circles; however, the suppression of information is mostly enforced for personal safety to protect targeted individuals from law enforcement.

This policy is statistically significant with domestic assassination and is correlated with capital punishment.

Capital punishment is implemented domestically when an individual has snitched on a fellow gang member to receive a lighter sentence or to avoid incarceration and results in the other party receiving a lengthy sentence. It is easy to implement this policy but difficult to enforce because the informant will usually receive protective custody, relocation, and change of identity.

The policy can usually be enforced if the informant remains in prison with the general population or if he returns to the same community, but sometimes the informant can receive a pardon by the city council, mayor, and constituents due to general consensus. Capital punishment usually requires paperwork or written documentation providing statements and accusations the informant has made.

Economic policies revolve around fiscal policy and the national tax system. Fiscal policy is the change in government expenditures and taxes to alter economic variables. Chapter 5 illustrated street gang expenditures which can increase rapidly due to crisis, conflict, or catastrophe. Healthcare initiatives have usually been unsuccessful because of the heavy tax burden it would impose on individuals.

Therefore, healthcare policies are only implemented during a time of crisis when a gang member has been wounded or murdered, and a car wash policy is always implemented immediately to raise funds for the victim and his family. Car washes take place in their territory immediately after an individual has been murdered and often times t-shirts and sweatshirts maintaining, "In loving memory of...," are worn and circulated, followed by candlelight vigils at the scene of the crime.

Another type of fiscal policy revolves around drug commerce and housing expenditures. During a time of crisis such as a raid or a seizure in which drugs are confiscated from a house/apartment/motel, revenues are expropriated and prevented from circulation; therefore, it is up to the city council members to help make up for a loss revenues by providing agricultural subsidies to some members (marijuana/drugs) to relocating drug commerce.

After a crisis has transpired, relocation of capital-intensive programs is necessary for the maintenance and revenues of the administration in the commercial environment, therefore working with special interest groups is necessary for the survival and sovereignty of the street gang organization.

Many gangs rely on a loose alliance and work with special interest groups who engage in drug trafficking or organized crime, and can mobilize product and resources from other countries or states, although this information is usually not transparent to the general public, and these special interests groups lobby street gang legislators to look out for their own best interest within the community.

It is common for individuals who are not members of the street gang organization who engage in drug commerce to be burdened with high tariffs for operating within their jurisdiction; however, there is usually diplomatic relations with these individuals because the relationship is codependent. The national tax system deals strictly with the tax burden and for every government action there is a public reaction because individuals engaged in capital-intensive industries will lobby city council members of street gangs to reduce their tax burden. Most gangs impose low taxes and provide low services.

All individual members in the gang are responsible for their own well-being such as food, clothing, medical care, education, employment, and shelter; therefore, domestic policies which serve the welfare of the citizenry are non-existent. The administration provides a low level of services because of the constant state of war and because the organizational culture is individual rather than communal, which means that even though they have a general-law community or practice fraternity and loyalty, it all seems to disappear when they become incarcerated.

Many individuals who go to jail or serve out a prison term feel as though everyone on the outside forgets about them because they rarely get visits or letters, however, life on the streets continues. The philosophy within the social contract has always left individual prisoners disenfranchised from the street gang on the outside because of its individualistic duality.

Street gang organizations do not provide social welfare programs, thus individuals are responsible for producing their own capital and are not provided with unemployment benefits, pension plans, or long-term social security. However, the street gang legislators pass policies which contribute to individual's civil liberties such as freedom of speech or association, and civil rights such as anti-discriminatory and minority rights.

Freedom of speech is fundamental to the idea of popular government because individuals must be able to participate in public debates or alternatives, which they also have the freedom to associate or petition the existing government. Individual gang members who are dissatisfied with the political climate can associate or petition the existing government, encourage change, and express their concerns without fear of repercussions, however sometimes dissident behavior is considered threatening.

Civil rights include anti-discriminatory policies which allow all members of the organization to have equal opportunities and to be able to compete, succeed, or enjoy as does any other member despite race, religion, or gender. Most gangs are homogenized organizations, yet there are sometimes a small percentage of women, atheists, Satanists, blacks, whites, Asians, and other Hispanics that are not of the dominant Mexican-American heritage which makes up the cultural demographic, thus their civil rights are protected under these types of policies.

Lastly, because of the constant state of war, a war policy is implemented amongst neighboring territories to determine behavior towards certain sovereignties. According to nation-states prior to the creation of the United Nations, a declaration of war is the most diplomatic and acceptable policy in regards to a state of hostilities between nations.

Any military engagement by a nation must be approved by its legislature, unless it is a clandestine operation, however when in war, there are laws nation-states must adhere to and certain responsibilities must be upheld. For example, neutral nations and civilians must be protected from hostile aggression and violence.

However, when laws are ignored by nation-states and crimes against humanity are present in the state of war, they could possibly be charged with war crimes and suffer repercussions amongst the international community. Most wars are about sovereignty, territory, resources, ethnicity, and other issues which are determined later in history, which is also the same for street gangs. All gangs in Los Angeles are engaged in urban warfare, therefore war policy is the most significant and effortless policy to implement and enforce.

Street gang legislatures do not have to approve military engagements because often a street conflict is random and impetuous, thus decisions must be made by those involved in the conflict. A basic example is when a small group of gang members or a sole individual is driving around, cruising, walking, shopping, partying, or just passing through a foreign territory, and although they are not looking for a conflict, another group of gang members who control that territory approaches them with hostility or aggression.

The standard policy is to "hit them up" or ask them where they are from to identify if the interrogators are familiar with the response or the name of their street gang. There is usually a strong possibility that the interrogators might respond with aggression by denouncing the opposing gang or simply with physical force because of their violent nature.

They might respond by asking what regional bloc they are from *vis-à-vis* the Los Angeles County, or ask if they have a problem with their neighborhood. Sometimes if the street gang location is too far, they will give them a pass, allow them as transients as long as they recognize the significant presence of the controlling street gang organization, and they must make sure to avoid aggressive behavior. Sometimes, it can result in a battleground as either party can respond with a physical reaction which can result in a street fight, hospitalization, or a murder.

As the blood-spattered boulevards shatter the war-torn communities, a counterattack or a showdown will supersede the previous incident and reinforce the constant state of war. In some situations, the perpetrators will actually go back to the crime scene out of cold-heartedness or curiosity to see how much infliction they have caused, and then they can report the news to headquarters, thus contributing to their fierce reputation to increase their war stripes.

In some circumstances, individuals can actually get caught by law enforcement agencies that have a description of the suspects. Street gang organizations have an open policy in regards to witnesses of crime, which can result in open execution or pressure on someone's well-being, thus resulting in a large percentage of deterrence in regards to reporting or identifying criminal activity.

This contributes to high-density level communities that digest hideous crimes and become somewhat immune to urban, unconventional warfare, thus the civilian population must also deal with random violence, sometimes also dealing with irrational or damaging psychological development.

War policy maintains that civilians should be protected from random shootings and murder, however when there is collateral damage, the perpetrators can be charged with crimes against humanity at the prison congress level and suffer repercussions with their own type of jurisprudence. Based on the hideousness of the crime, it will be assessed on a case-by-case analysis at the local level and the prison congress, resulting in anything from a slap on the wrist to capital punishment.

When dealing with gangs which are not neutral and are considered extreme enemies, the policy is usually to react rapidly and boldly during any conflict or on a mission during a military campaign. In street gang urban politics, a neutral gang does not mean that the regime does not engage in military combats.

A neutral gang refers to a street gang which does not conflict in military combats with transients or neighborhoods that are too far to wage a military campaign against. Street gangs are in a constant state of war with bordering territories because of the close proximity and the frequent run-ins with each other that lead to small battles, fights, or rumbles, all of which can be considered asymmetric and guerrilla warfare, which often end in bloodshed.

As in any war, the history behind the feud remains biased or ambiguous, therefore a formal declaration was never imposed, but the perennial military conflict will continue because of bloodshed. What is important to remember is that when somebody is murdered in street warfare, it is always someone's brother, cousin, uncle, friend, or neighbor, so retaliation will always be expected. Because the enemy is so close, it will render a personal vendetta, sustaining the hostility for years.

Because street gang organizations are so spread out and they usurp territory in numerous cities and communities, a state of widespread panic and conflict exists in the Los Angeles County, which can be considered a battle zone where combatants engage in constant military campaigns. In traditional war theory, urbanized communities are easier to defend than open spaces because there are plenty of places to hide and wait for enemy activity such as buildings, cars, and trees. Coincidentally, these same factors make it easier for adversaries to use the element of surprise and launch a deadly assault.

Although the social contract is supposed to provide individual gang members with protection from foreign invasion and peace within their jurisdiction, most individual gang members are in a constant state of fear. The fear cannot be transparent because it is destructive in combat, however they all feel it but suppress it because it is contagious and can cause low morale or panic amongst a multitude. Most individual gang members are confined to provincialism and stay within their jurisdiction because of the fear of violent death or murder.

When traveling for recreational and miscellaneous purposes, they try to stay in territories which do not have a significant gang presence; otherwise they increase their chances of being exposed to fear or the suffering of reprisals. Individual gang members prefer comrade assistance when traveling, or they take a weapon to protect themselves. They are constantly looking over their shoulders because they actually fear death, yet they masquerade fearlessness, they are consumed by pride, and most will defend their sovereign state with fights or battles that give them excitement or an adrenaline rush.

A simple glance or stare can result in aggressive behavior because gang members maintain loads of anger and frustration. Therefore, if a group or individual is wearing traditional street gang clothing, if they are staring with hard looks, or if they are driving traditional street gang culture vehicles, they can quickly become engaged in a showdown which contributes to the cyclical street warfare.

Although urban warfare maintains a clear policy on separation of church and state to avoid a social dichotomy, the duality of man will nevertheless exist due to his psychology *vis-à-vis* the state of war, which is a perennial phenomenon. Because the state of nature is anarchic, mankind has a natural instinct and inherent violent character that is amplified and becomes an outlet during the state of war.

In urban communities that are plagued with street gang organizations, sometimes street warfare is a way to channel the alienation, apathy, disillusionment, or anxiety that is caused by the social dichotomy. The Mexican-American must learn to cope with an identity crisis that internally forces him to be defensive, skeptical, and nationalistic, while simultaneously dealing with outside factors that force him to externally assimilate, embrace, and self-loathe.

American history has inadvertently taught that the Mexican is illegal, criminal, and antisocial; therefore, this type of behavior is unequivocally expected in the social spectrum, which sometimes furnishes a form of self-loathing.

The self-loathing is displaced and projected against others who look similar and those who adhere to the same philosophy, which is the phenomenon of street warfare. They are left with constant frustration while they fight for their soul between good and evil. Some would argue that war is innate and part of the necessary evolution of mankind, however, the state of war that exists at the street level is a clear extension of animal instincts such as: territory, competition, and sovereignty, which is reflective of nation-states that have gone to war.

The transformation is psychologically damaging and irrational to self-development, thus the duality of man is amplified during a state of war. They are in a constant battle between themselves as they become polarized between positive and negative frictions, therefore, the rival street gang organization has become the legitimized enemy and they are prevented from seeing the real enemies, which is them.

CHAPTER 7: CONGRESS AND COUNTY GOVERNMENTS

The California Senate is structured as a bicameral legislature with two houses including an upper house the state senate, and a lower house, the state assembly. The Congress meets on a year round basis in the state capital of Sacramento, and its legislators are elected from district boundaries which are defined by the U.S. Census Bureau. State senators can serve two terms that last four years, while assemblymen can serve three terms that last six years.

The main presiding officers in the California congress include: a lieutenant governor for the state senate, a floor speaker for the state assembly, and the governor who oversees the legislature and who has ultimate executive authority. Most of the work in the legislature is conducted by standing committees, assigned by the speaker, and the Rules Committee appoints all members to all committees, which makes it the governing committee.

There are many committees and issues in the state of California because of its physical size, which results in a divided, polarized government. Because of the many differences between Northern and Southern California, a significant polarization exists within the legislature. In order for a bill to become a law, it is first introduced by a legislator to the assembly or the senate, and then it goes to one or more standing committees for consideration.

The committees will then decide an action to take, such as amending the bill or reporting the bill to the other chamber for amendment and debate. If the bill is accepted without changes, it goes to the governor for ratification, if not it goes back to the original chamber. When it finally reaches the governor it is either accepted or vetoed.

The state legislature has three functions that include: 1.) Policymaking, which is executing laws and distributing funds. 2.) Representation of the citizenry, which includes the constituency from districts and boundaries. 3.) Oversight, which is performance of administration of local/county governments.

The California congress has formal structures; however, it also has informal norms and unwritten policies such as: emphasizing tenure or superiority of seniority, paying dues for rookies, cue-taking based on partisanship, interest group pressures, arguments and alignment with other legislators, personal agendas or what their conscience dictates, and the behavior of the governor.

The state legislature is also responsible for setting up county governments that function as satellite government locations for the state to provide services to residents of certain jurisdictions or boundaries. The counties are made up of boards of supervisors usually led by a chief financial officer to assist in the day-to-day activities and administration.

The board of supervisors appoints department heads and commission members, yet it also shares executive authority with three independently elected officials including: the Sheriff, the District Attorney, and the Assessor. The county is responsible for providing public services such as: social services, healthcare, public protection, public works, regulating land use and development, voting rights, welfare, tax assessment and collection, waste management, and other services through the courts and jails.

Within Mexican-American gangs, the prison system functions as the state congress with a bicameral legislature with two houses known as the Southside, the upper house/senate, and the Northside, the lower house/state assembly. The congress is made up of mostly Southside or Southernist senators who are warehoused in Pelican Bay, many in the secure housing unit (SHU). On the outside, the Sureño sphere of influence extends to the Central Coast and includes the counties of San Luis Obispo, Kern, Santa Barbara, and around Los Angeles like Ventura, San Bernardino, Orange, Riverside, San Diego, and Imperial.

The members who make up the prison system congress are picked up in different districts throughout the state to carry out congressional terms for conducting criminal activities, thus they represent districts and boundaries which make up their street gang and regional bloc. There are no term limits for prison legislators because some can serve as little as a year, while some can have lifetime tenure by carrying out a life sentence in the SHU.

Serving a prison term for conducting criminal activity within a street gang does not automatically make someone a Southside senator or a Northside assemblyman. Membership in the prison congress depends on street credibility, reputation in the prison

73

system, and political behavior, therefore, it is a lengthy process to join the prison congress. Additionally, several of the career congressmen are serving long prison terms, thus membership is usually accepted after years of experience.

Due to its very nature of secrecy and conspiracy, the prison congress is a clandestine organization that executes policies amongst the general population, it allocates funds to its constituency, it represents outside districts and regional blocs although the prison congress has overall authority, and it provides oversight to its county administrations and outside street gangs. Most of the legislation done in the prison congress is also done in standing committees and hearings, however, the Southside senators and Northside assemblymen are completely polarized in the industrial prison complex, thus a perennial civil war has resulted with sporadic bargaining and negotiating.

The prison congress is responsible for setting up satellite locations in different prisons in order to enforce policy and implementation; therefore, the prison congress also has county governments that function as extensions of the congress throughout the state of California.

Currently the state of California has thirty-two state prisons and fifty-eight county governments; therefore, in reference to the prison congress, there are thirty-one satellite governments which include: Wasco, Avenal, Calipatria, Centinela, Tehachapi, Corona, San Luis Obispo, Norco, Jamestown, Chuckwalla, Tracy, Folsom, Ironwood, Los Angeles County, Ione, Delano, Pelican Bay, Pleasant valley, San Diego, New

Folsom, and San Quentin, while Susanville, Corcoran, Chowchilla, Vacaville, and Soledad each have two prisons. The county/satellite prisons are run by a board of supervisors like a county government and a chief financial officer who is the main figurehead or shot-caller.

However, a conventional county government also has three independently elected officials including: the Sheriff, the Assessor, and District Attorney, but in each prison the main shot-caller functions as all of those roles. He has complete judicial, legislative, and executive authority over the prison populace which gives him the power to execute jurisprudence such as crime and punishment, implement and execute policies, maintain deputies/soldiers, collect taxes, distribute funds, and allocate resources. The shot-caller is appointed by the prison congress based on political reputation and tenure, but usually the position cannot be filled by a rookie because of the informal rule of seniority.

Each prison is run by a chief financial officer, the shot-caller, with the assistance of a board of supervisors who are responsible for a district, which in prison is considered a yard. There are usually four to five yards per prison, therefore, each prison has about four or five supervisors who assist with the day-to-day activities of the prison and appoint department heads to run each building that are labeled from A to E. Moreover, department heads assign staff assistants to run each level in the building, which are tiers, and usually the complete cycle of assigning public positions is based on patronage, an informal norm within the prison system congress.

The industrial prison complex is informally set up as a learning institute for political socialization of the recidivism philosophy. Juvenile Halls are considered elementary schools, California Youth Authorities are considered high schools, County jails are considered community colleges, and state prisons are considered universities although some are referenced as gladiator schools because of the extreme demands it takes to survive. Ultimately, the prison congress would be the career criminal/politician. Street gang organizations on the outside are politically socialized with war theory and engage in consistent battles with adverse enemies within their close proximities. However, when entering the prison system for the first time through juvenile hall, an inmate quickly learns to practice tolerance, solidarity, and fraternity with all Southernist Hispanic gang members.

The main policy passed by the prison congress is ethnic identification and solidarity; however, there are a small percentage of inmates who represent a different ethnic group rather than their own because the strong affiliation which they have adopted within their social contract transcends ethnic boundaries. Even though inmates and cellmates represent opposing gangs on the outside and they could possibly be imprisoned for murdering an enemy, they must practice solidarity as a legislative policy.

Occasionally, some inmates will request a personal feud and there are occasional individual feuds, however, most join the status-quo. Segregation is the most significant policy in the prison system because all formal policies and unwritten norms come from the division of ethnic groups which is another means of protection within the social contract. In other words, all inmates are competing for a scarcity of resources and power within a social contract but now within a different environment than on the streets.

When an individual first enters the industrial prison complex, it is as though he is an immigrant in a war torn battle zone. Now he must learn the art of war in order to survive. When a gang member on the outside is engaged in street warfare, it is easier to not get involved because he has an option to renounce membership or stay home and avoid danger; however, when engaged in prison warfare, there are no options because he must consistently engage in asymmetric warfare.

Within the prison system, the war is much closer than on the outside. There is nowhere to hide, you cannot stay in your cell, and you will have to 'put in work' or suffer repercussions which will leave you ostracized. Those who decide to renounce their involvement in prison politics and prison warfare end up in protective custody with the worst reputation following them around forever, which leaves them in a constant state of alienated flux.

Prison policies mandate constant war and segregation amongst Hispanics, whites, and blacks; however, the Hispanics, mostly Mexican-Americans, are also engaged in a perennial civil war amongst the Southernist blue coats/bandanas from Southern California, and the Northside red coats/bandanas from Northern California. (*Sureños* and *Norteños*)

The civil war manifests itself in the form of stabbings, murders, and scheduled/random battles which are reflective of medieval battles because it is a tense war of all against all using homemade weapons. The riots are usually between the Southern and Northern Hispanics, or between the Southern Hispanics and the Blacks.

The Southern Hispanics have created a truce agreement with some of the Caucasian prison gangs including The Aryan Brotherhood, Armenian Power, *and* the Nazi Low-rider's, even though they represent a small percentage of the prison population, because they have both maintained a perennial conflict with the Black prison gangs.

On the other hand, the Northern Hispanics commonly have friendly relations with the Black prison gangs, further contributing to their polarized prison congress. Usually, the Southern Hispanics have more soldiers who will fight to the bitter end because they have more heart and discipline, but also because they fear reprisals from their own, while the Northern Hispanics and the Blacks usually retreat.

What results is a divided prison population which is engaged in an intense civil war, they are divided by absolute segregation, they are involved in consistent feuds amongst different ethnic populations, and they render absolute discipline and solidarity within their ethnic groups. This type of political socialization is reinforced on a daily basis because people are directly influenced by the ecology of their environment, thus, it is difficult not to succumb to this type of institutionalism, hence the recidivism philosophy.

The recidivism philosophy exists because inmates have become politically socialized in the prison system where certain behaviors, rules, and conduct are the norm, however, when they join the real world on the outside they cannot adjust to the rules and norms. They simply continue the criminal behavior that landed them in prison in the first place because sometimes their life is more manageable in prison.

When some inmates are released from prison to join the real world, a sense of schizophrenia exists because they can become completely polarized by an overwhelming world which looks at ex-convicts as substandard humans. Society in general including: family members, employers, law enforcement, friends, neighbors, women they try to court, etc…can contribute to their schizophrenia because society harshly judges people with a magnifying glass, which most often they are refused employment opportunities. Therefore, the ex-convict feels as though he cannot contribute to society nor function as a civil human being within his community, thus he has become a statistical product of his environment.

In the prison system, categories of good and evil simply cease to control behavior; thus many inmates do not feel judged because they are not physically present in contemporary society. When entering the industrial prison complex, inmates must wear a warrior mask in order to promote bravado behavior or be labeled a coward.

No matter how old you are, you must consistently prove your courage even though the inner anguish or suffering could become overwhelming. Several inmates feel completely disconnected from humanity without any attachment to reality. Some do not renounce the moral laws which judged them because they seek out salvation or forgiveness in the form of prayer, in turn some also suffer repercussions from other inmates who look at those who seek out theology as desperate vulnerability. Most inmates are cognizant that their alienation or consequences are a direct result of their choices, but the sub-standard living conditions of the prison system leave them with a sense of a broken soul and regression.

When first entering the prison system as a teenager in juvenile hall, the humiliation and embarrassment of stripping clothes, the insecurity about their genitals or anatomy, the showering with five to ten inmates with small towels, the lack of sufficient fitted clothing, the use of plastic pillows for comfort, and the adjustment to unflavored, insignificant portions of food would make anyone recoil and wish they were at home. However, the fear of the unknown becomes routine after inmates learn to adapt to their environment even though they are nostalgic about the outside world and ponder their detached existence from a world which was once familiar.

The nostalgia soon becomes suppressed because it makes them vulnerable to weakness, thus they must learn to compartmentalize their depression, live in a bleak existence, and wear a warrior mask with a superhuman cape at all times. Moreover, there is a marginalized group of inmates who suffer much more social stratification which are the homosexuals, who are manipulated or coerced into providing domestic, sexual, and financial obligations.

As inmates are released from prison but then succumb to the recidivism philosophy, the dark side of humanity seems like a familiar place but the fear of the unknown ceases to exist. When they reenter the prison system they learn to auto desensitize and mentally prepare themselves for the prison politics and inhumane living conditions that lie ahead. Some make themselves believe they could have a meaningful existence amongst the prison population because of their knowledge, skills, and abilities within the organizational culture of prison, seeking to become career politicians. Others become disillusioned by the organizational culture and begin to loathe themselves, the prison system, the prison congress, and other inmates because of its redundancy and social order.

CHAPTER 8: THE UNDERGROUND MEDIA

In the United States, the media is protected by the First Amendment which upholds the freedom of the press. The media is supposed to be neutral and independent, and it is supposed to provide the public with information that is necessary, interesting, essential, and it should be reported without bias. There are many mediums of obtaining public information including: newspapers, magazines, newsletters, television, radio, cable satellite, internet, and word-of-mouth.

In today's society, modern technology has replaced the way people procure political information from print newspapers to prime time network news channels to smart phones. Print information such as newspapers and magazines are in direct competition with internet sources like online blogs and social media networks. Therefore, those in the underground get information through all mediums of communication, including word-of-mouth, alternative methods, and modern technology.

Print information is more complex because the reader can interpret the information based on his/her assessment, while television reporting focuses on people's emotional spectrum; it is less complex in delivery and interpretation of ideas, pandering to people's desire for scandal, gossip, and conflict. Furthermore, Marshal McLuhan declares that there are many ways of communicating with the masses, and that those mediums of communication shape their ideas, thoughts, or actions because they subtly alter our perceptual senses, and because the medium itself is the message.

He maintains that all technologies are extensions of mankind, and that our central nervous system is super-stimulated because of the pseudo-environment created by different mediums of communication. Some of those other mediums of communication include: speech, dress, infrastructure, artwork, and technology.

All mediums of communication help shape people's lives because of the phenomenon or dogma created and associated with different paradigms such as: religious fanaticism, neo-liberal capitalism, or collective racism. Street gang organizations use many types of mediums of communication to produce a collective militarism which reinforces the socialization of street gang behavior and as a propagandist ideology. Within street gangs, the medium is the message because they cannot use the popular mediums of communication to get in touch with the masses.

Politicians also use the mass media as a tool to communicate with the general public and their constituencies through expensive spot advertisements or rehearsed speeches. During political campaigns, the mass media covers less information in regards to policy matters, major events, and leadership concerns, and more information on politician's private lives, extramarital affairs, scandal, gossip, and any other type of information that is sensationalized and interpreted as conflicting or dramatic.

As a result, the public is cynical, unsympathetic, and disillusioned by political journalism because of its lack of essential information, and its abundant reporting on dramatic or incident-based events. Many view the political process as entertainment or sport. Large percentages of the citizenry view national elections as horse races, rather than elections, thus resulting in low voter turnout and apolitical behavior.

According to some media experts, the media is neither objective nor responsive, which is also considered to have an ideological and professional bias, but it depends on who interprets the bias. Some experts believe that conservative critics often point to studies that show that the majority of national news reporters are Democratic, liberal, and urban-oriented. Some point to the influence of conservative corporate executives who oversee the communications empires of radio stations, newspapers, and television networks. And still, some look to the corporate interests that advertise on these media and contribute to their profits and to the editorials that reflect the conservative views of the owners, publishers, and advertisers.

Some media experts also maintain that academic observers perceive a professional bias where the media reports whatever is interesting to most people all the time because it is soft, sensational, and dramatic, and it attracts more viewers, yet it is not accurate or informative; it is not essential to an educated public and electorate. What results is a media which reports incomplete and sensational information that caters to people's emotions, includes ideological polarization of reporting that is either too liberal or too conservative, it expresses a professional journalism that is skewed based on reporters' ideas of what is newsworthy, personal ideology, and the amount of audience interest.

Nevertheless, it is important to remember that the constitution protects the freedom of the press, which is objective and neutral, which is owned by billion dollar multinational corporations joined continuously by conglomerate mergers, which dominate the mediums of communication and the airwaves that shift the political culture and ideology of the masses.

Due to the political culture of street gangs, gang members use alternative mediums of communication with a political slant, and informally create a pseudo-environment based on a propagandist ideology. Gang members in public office also lose their private status and the street media becomes involved with their private lives, extramarital affairs, scandal, gossip, and anything else that is considered dramatically conflicting. This chapter will examine the mediums of communication which street gang organizations use throughout the underground circles to alter the perpetual habits of the masses.

Within the social contract, the media is not used by corporate advertisers to buy consumers, but it is used as a propagandist ideology that reinforces the political socialization of street gang culture. Instead of buying consumers, street gangs buy enlistment, fear, and retention. Underground street media is conveyed orally through the grapevine and invokes the power of speech or rhetoric to capture audience attention. In the unincorporated community of Lennox, the radical faction of the far left coined the street media 'The Lennox Loudspeaker,' taken from a monthly newsletter which was published at the Lennox Middle School they attended as children. It is juxtaposed as satire due to its swift travel through the grapevine.

Street gangs are almost always interested in expansion, thus they campaign year round through word-of-mouth like tribal and oral cultures to improve enrollment and reduce turnover rates. Their target audience shares the same demographics, thus the public image is considered reflective representation of the constituency, which is striking to impressionable adolescents who are considering enrollment. Many street gang members use intense grassroots campaigning by seeking support from its residents in the form of persuasion or brainwashing through redundant advertisement. Although they do not use television, radio, or other popular mediums of communication, street gangs use spot advertisements on the street to communicate with the general public and their constituencies at local conventions, informal caucuses, public hang outs, or school facilities.

Street gangs use wall space like advertisements and political slogans by vandalizing walls with graffiti that depicts their sovereign state to promote against opposing factions or other gangs, and to communicate powerful corporate images like the number 13, the Southernist prison ideology, and hand signs to elicit mysticism or reverence. The graffiti itself is an antisocial behavior that allows the content and cryptic messages to be effective communication tools of underground street media where the medium is the message. Moreover, graffiti style is associated with social class, thus gang members who usually vandalize with abstract style and innovation are considered middle-class, while those that misspell words or lack creativity are considered working-class.

Within street gang organizations, class conflict is ostensibly de-emphasized and is not supposed to be a salient theme, however, many gangs or cliques consider immigration policies and how it will contribute to their public image. Many gangs who do not have a flux of recent immigrants denounce other gangs which do by insulting them with derogatory terms adopted by mainstream society.

In street gangs, factions/political parties are sometimes created around socio-economic status and help contribute to the division of government within their own street gang organization. This class conflict that is sensationalized through the underground street media often contributes to factionalism or internal feuding that sometimes exists. Although this problem probably exists within many gangs, it is de-emphasized to avoid rendering speculation of division of government to outside observers, and sensationalism throughout the underground street media.

Speech and dress are also associated with social-economic status, class conflict, and mediums of communication. Many gang members who are first, second, or third generation, many who have immigrant parents but were raised in an English-speaking environment, or those who have mastered the English language, have more confidence in addressing an audience or establishing diplomatic relations. On the other hand, those who speak with an accent, those who have immigrated and have a limited education, and those who simply cannot or refuse to master the English language, lack confidence and succumb to coyness. They do not usually participate in diplomatic or public relations, they do not normally hold high public office, and they usually join the constituency because of pressure groups or the desire to fit into a strange world.

Furthermore, these gang members use back-slang which combines English and Spanish, which results in a simple, yet unconventional dialect that uses trickery and smooth talk to alter perception. Marshall McLuhan maintains that, "Slang offers immediate index to changing perception that is based on immediate experience and new perpetual habits." In other words, when back-slang is conveyed and exchanged amongst individuals, there is immediate participation amongst them because they have engaged in an altered perception which becomes training for a new habit of conversing.

Moreover, when a gang member uses an open platform to address an audience, the entire audience is immediately participating in an altered perception because they are completely involved with trained habit. Once again, the medium is the message because the altered speech itself is an effective communication tool adopted by street gangs as an antisocial method that invokes a collective consciousness. Thus, mastering back-slang effectively with proper English fluency is positively correlated with socio-economic status, and it can contribute to class conflict.

Although street gang organization dress code is extremely similar and is meant to be duplicated, the way they wear the clothes, their grooming habits, their jewelry, and their pressing habits, also contribute to socio-economic status, class conflict, and mediums of communication.

Gang members who come from a middle-class background wear their clothes with more fashion and finesse than those from the working-class. Middle-class gang members put more thought into their wardrobe such as: constantly keeping up with the latest fashion trends in popular culture, maintaining clean sneakers, pressing their khakis/jeans/shorts to uphold appearances, exhibiting self-sufficient and clean grooming techniques, showing off jewelry that is significant with wealth, demonstrating a variety of articles such as hats, sports jackets, jerseys, sneakers, button-ups, polo shirts, and anything else they wear to show off their surplus wardrobe.

Working-class gang members do not put much thought into their dress code and wear the usual solid colors or conspicuous clothing articles, yet they lack fashion and creativity in regards to style. Class conflict can be physically observed through the act of maintaining a 'clean look,' which is overemphasized in street gang organizations to substantiate the sovereign's public image.

The dress code in general communicates an antisocial behavior as a means to identify with a certain lifestyle, or to demonstrate solidarity, uniformity, and equality amongst themselves. It is meant to be conspicuous; it is a medium of resistance against the consumerist status-quo, the typical rat race, and the standardized behavior of the masses.

Street gang members cannot meet the demands of the general population or the typical technologies, thus they become non-conformists and seemingly irrational to the homogenized linear thinker. The dress code transforms commonplace perception because it trains people and forces them to associate lifestyle and behavior with dress, consequently communicating a powerful message of propagandist ideology.

Another popular medium of communication throughout the underground media is urban artwork in the form of drawings, art, lettering, and lyricism. Street art is considered lowbrow due to its uncultivated framework, illegal vandalism, subversive inscriptions, and lack of coloring schemes; however, this type of subversive artwork is not a new phenomenon and is deeply rooted in the ancient civilizations of: Greece, the Roman Empire, Egypt, Turkey, Constantinople, and Mesoamerica.

Many cultures throughout time have expressed their interpretation of the world through antisocial artwork including graffiti and illegal vandalism on public and private surfaces, thus contemporary street gangs have adopted the same ritual. They use public or private surfaces to mark territory and publicly display a significant presence of gang activity, which is challenging to the status-quo and its linear perception.

Most urban artwork in street gang organizations is directly influenced by prison life, street struggle and survival, and subconscious surrealism. Engaging in creative artwork is a form of escapism for gang members in prison or on the street, relying on exotic imagery that is revealed through the subconscious mind and exists outside of reason or aesthetic perception, which is characteristic of the surrealist movement.

As was mentioned, street gang organizations and secret societies are notorious for abusing drugs and alcohol to produce ecstasy and enhanced mental states, which allows for creative imagination and perception of street life artistry that reflects: anxiety, apathy, and alienation. Also, the commonplace street gang tattoos which serve as iconic propagandist images that can be duplicated by all gang members to demonstrate uniformity or duplication of a collective consciousness. Gang members use their bodies as billboards for political campaigning and promotion for their sovereign state, regional bloc, and the prison senate by tattooing themselves with street gang imagery which challenges the status-quo.

Those within the artistic community of street gangs execute their work by tattooing, writing on walls, on letters from prison, and other miscellaneous items, however, most will never have a show at an art gallery, or a tattoo shop to promote their artistic abilities. In the late '80's and early '90's, two magazines known as Teen Angel and Lowrider Magazine allowed those within the street gang culture and artist community to submit photographs, paintings, drawings, sculptures, and other such works to be considered for recognizable distinction.

Those magazines were used to target a specific audience, which was the street gang culture, and to expedite communication to different regional blocs by merely having a visual impact which sparked curiosity. Lowrider Magazine still exists today and has also found a new target audience in Yokohoma, Japan, which results in a cultural exchange because of the presence of the U.S. Navy base, thus the city has

91

become influenced by the lowrider phenomenon. Urban artwork alters and trains perception like any other art movement, but forces the populace to look at their artwork through a lens of realism and despair, rather than judge it as a consumer commodity or as trained professional art historians or critics.

Another type of artwork adopted by street gang organizations is the lyrical rhyming influenced by the hip hop community which facilitates communication amongst a multitude through street dialogue that includes: back-slang rhyming, folk tales, denunciation of rival gangs, and mastery of manipulation over hardcore instrumental beats. Traditional street gang lyricists rhyme about war stories, territorial landmarks, love of sovereignty, debauchery, licentious behavior, or excessive denouncement that compels rival lyricists to retaliate.

Many underground lyrical artists in the early '90's came out of the Westside, which contributed to the underground street raps that dominated the art community and contributed to the propagandist ideology. Some of those artists flourished with popularity and prestige during the early 90's and climaxed during the Renaissance of the Westside regional bloc. (See Chapter 12) The underground street media would circulate these works to the citizenry which would later become known as the 'Westside Raps' and became extremely coveted by street gang members, the general public, and by the artists themselves.

During the Westside Renaissance, a group of troubadours from the unincorporated community of Lennox introduced an unconventional style of lyricism that was directly influenced by the Wu-Tang Clan from New York, and NWA (Niggaz with Attitude) from Los Angeles, which resulted in a fusion of conventional hardcore street folk tales, merged with creative style and design which emphasized: impressive vocabulary, highly methodical capabilities, duality of self, and worldwide social concerns.

The group of troubadours created their own instrumental beats which were often influenced by classical chamber music, gothic/dark wave rock, traditional hardcore/gangster beats, and world music from Latin America, while the lyrical content and style were influenced by civil philosophers, east coast/west coast rappers, religious theology, and other ideologies that help shape world opinions.

This group was known as 'The Post Meridians', and although they never released any material on a popular or independent label, they did record music at professional recording studios and did promotional work for Julio G. (92.3 The Beat), a demo that was never released, they had radio play at a local underground radio station (88.9 KXLU), and their cassettes and CD's still circulate throughout the Lennox underground today.

Infrastructure also has a positive correlation between oral underground media and street gang organizations. Information conveyed through the grapevine can be facilitated through streets or highways that make it more accessible for those within the street gang culture to travel to new locations. During the early '90's when the 105 freeway became accessible, gang members from the Westside found it easier to travel to areas such as: the Harbor Area, East

Los Angeles, Downtown/Central Los Angeles, the Northeast, and South Los Angeles/South Central.

Many of those areas had cruising locations, which were sanctuaries for gang activity, such as: Laurel Canyon in San Fernando, Hollywood Blvd in the Central Los Angeles area, Whittier Blvd in East Los Angeles, and Bristol St in Orange County. These locations provided informal conventions where street gang members could demonstrate their flags, their cars, or their significant presence. It also increased the barometer to get involved in conflicting battle zones, but they could also meet women from different areas, which was usually the sole purpose for congregating in those areas.

One of the main reasons why gang members travel to unknown locations is to meet or party with women from different regions, which is related to their debauchery, but it also contributes to conflicts of interest with other street gangs. When women party or frequent with gang members, they often invite them to gatherings in foreign neighborhoods, despite the fact that it could be a hostile or neutral territory, which exposes those gang members in volatile unchartered areas.

The gang member or members who are traveling abroad can find themselves at a party, a club, a gathering, or any other public place which might allow them to get caught in a difficult situation without a hospitable welcome. Women play a significant role within the underground media because they gossip about scandal, drama, and gang member's public or private lives to friends and relatives, thus news stories begin to circulate within the underground community.

94

People in general, including street gang members, have an overall consensus of pleasure to be around the masses and feel as though they are part of a community or something bigger than themselves. There is a power in numbers that gang members subscribe to, whether it is their own street gang organization, or in community conventions like car shows, cruising spots, or festivals.

Marshal McLuhan maintains that it is a magically subconscious awareness to be around the masses and alter our senses to this medium of communication. To be part of a collective consciousness is to be part of a global community, regardless if it is subversive, thus many people do not want to pass up the opportunity to belong to an ideology that is bigger than them.

Marshal McLuhan professes that the central nervous system becomes super-stimulated in a complex urban social experience, because of the pseudo-environment created by different mediums of communication. Individuals in street gangs have a super-stimulated central nervous system because of the complex state of war in their neighborhoods, and because of the different mediums of communication that reinforce the propagandist ideology of the street gang culture. The central nervous system becomes desensitized to the complex violence experienced, therefore, it learns to cope and compartmentalize actions or reactions.

The central nervous system commands all physical activities, while stimulating mental consciousness; therefore, it becomes super-stimulated because the social experiences are overwhelming. When the central nervous system becomes exposed to this type of stimulation, it must succumb to numbness or it will result in extreme polarization of the mind. The social order and structure of street gang organizations forces gang members to numb themselves to the policies and procedures of the organizational culture, thereby adopting the violent behavior that comes with the social contract.

When joining the social contract, the central nervous system must decolonize itself from practical actions and reactions, and learn a complex method of responding to stimuli. Outside observers and the citizenry living within street gang organization boundaries also become infected through the central nervous system because they must also respond differently to the policies and procedures adopted by them. Because they live in a constant atmosphere of gang activity, they must also succumb to numbness and respond to stimuli in a different way.

The general public responds differently to violent crimes that are witnessed because of the jurisprudence which they enforce, and because the well-being of civilians is not protected in street gang territories. The underground media attacks the central nervous system through all mediums of communication, including technology, because it forces people to respond differently to the super-stimulation in their complex pseudo-environment.

Marshal McLuhan says that all technologies are extensions of ourselves, which makes us become stimulated by them, therefore, we embrace technologies through a narcissistic fashion. We embrace our technologies, they are extensions of ourselves, and we serve some objects or technologies because they become natural to our existence. Some of these objects become extensions of us and it seems as though they cannot be separated because they are one and the same with mankind.

Men have always had a sexual relationship to the motorcar and people in general talk about having dream cars. Street gang members are no different in this respect so they also have a sexual relationship to the motorcar. There are certain vehicles which are associated with street gang culture, therefore in this analysis those motorcars can be associated with government vehicles. Gangsters become obsessed with certain vehicles and have them look a certain way to convey the propagandist ideology.

For example: a Cutlass Supreme or Buick Regal with a European front end, Luxury and Super Sport Monte Carlo, El Camino, Chevrolet Impala, Cadillac, etc…and others, which usually range anywhere from the 1960's to the present which sometimes include whitewalls, lowered with rims, a sound system, or a stock vehicle. The vehicle becomes an extension of the driver and turns him into a superhuman, which allows him to invoke an image similar to the knight errant with horse and armor.

Owning this type of vehicle can give the driver super status and empowerment, which allows these individuals to serve this object of technology with great reverence. Government vehicles are coveted by gang members because they help reinforce the street gang culture by being tools of communication through standardized repeatability.

Another technology that is an extension of mankind and is an object of obsession for the gang member is the gun. Street gangs are in a constant state of war, so weaponry is also an important object of technology. The philosophy of street gangs is to "live and die by the gun," so it is commonplace for gang members to get tattoos of weaponry on their bodies. Weaponry plays a strong and significant role because individuals serve those objects with great reverence.

It gives them superhuman powers that other technologies are incapable of. Many individual gang members even feel naked without their vehicle or weapon and feel as if they cannot function with their missing technologies. For street gang members, these technologies are extensions of them, they are mediums of communication, and they help reinforce the propagandist ideology.

When gang members come up to the surface from the underground, they discover that the popular media demonizes their culture, but simultaneously promotes their mysticism and awe. Coincidentally, the United States citizenry has always had an obsession with gang culture since their fascination with bootleg gangsters from the '20's, to the contemporary interpretation of street gang culture.

Popular mediums of communication such as: television shows, films, network news channels, documentaries, radio, internet, newspapers, and books have all contributed to the romanticism and glorification of gang culture.

During the early '90's and still today, Fox 11 news uses a reporter, Chris Blatchford, who investigates street gangs and other countercultures. Periodically he has news specials that assess the dramatic conflict of street gangs and their personal lives. He also wrote a book, 'The Black Hand' about Mexican Mafia dropout, Rene 'Boxer' Enriquez. Chris Blatchford specializes in sound bites designed to capture public attention. He has his target audience glued to the television to stay tuned for exhilarating war stories or information in general about street gang urban politics.

Chris Blatchford uses live footage which exposes counterculture activity, thus he caters to people's emotional spectrum by taking their lifestyle and putting it under a magnifying glass. Those who participate in counterculture activity, those who live in gang-infested communities, those who have family members in that kind of lifestyle, and anyone who has become socialized to their existence has a sympathetic yet scornful dual approach to street gang organizations.

Watching news specials about prison riots, urban warfare, and individual lives of those in gangs, helps gang members appear emotionally humane; because it often shows how they are conflicted by the social contract they have joined. Chris Blatchford's voice caters to people's sensitivity by stimulating their senses visually by demonstrating gang member's hard exterior surface, then following a storyline that involves conflict and scandal with a plea for understanding and compassion.

Another popular medium of communication that romanticizes street gang culture is the film industry. Films contribute to the glorification/demonization of Los Angeles County street gang culture by taking their lifestyle and putting it on the big screen, while catering to an international audience. Gangster films have usually done well domestically and internationally at the box office.

Moreover, some of the fictional/non-fictional superhuman characters depicted in those films have generated an obsession with their personalities such as: Scarface, The Godfather, Keyser Soze, Al Capone, and John Gotti. Gangster films appeal to those engaged in counterculture activity because it validates their subversive lifestyle; therefore, the message becomes skewed to the extent that it gives them the false hope of believing they can live a life of fast cash, women, and material possessions, while rendering prestige and respect amongst their peers.

Gangster films have directly influenced many individuals in the hip hop community who adopt gangster pseudonyms, lifestyles, style of dress, and merge it with their own microcosmic urban struggle using it in their songs, videos, or films.

Some rap artists have taken the streets to the stage and sell their urban lifestyle, struggle, or hustle, to mainstream multicultural America and international communities. Rap moguls Eazy E, Tupac Shakur, Biggie Smalls, and Duke of Psycho Realm have all suffered fatalities which were caused by their street life philosophy.

In the early '90's, a bicoastal feud began between west/east coast rappers that revolved around contravene verses, women, differences in lifestyle, dress, and other mediums of communication adopted by the differences between Los Angeles and New York. The bicoastal feud resulted in stabbings, shootings, jail sentences, and some murders, which were triggered by overt hostile aggression, and the

100

sensationalized drama that the popular media exploited because of the conflict, gossip, and scandal.

Other popular mediums of communication that glorify street gang or prison culture include: 'The Homies' toy line depicting gang members and the street culture, websites and blogs, popular clothing brands, some tattoo and graffiti artists, television commercials that use elements of gang culture, video games that depict street gangs and urban lifestyles, and popular television shows that explore gang culture with an empathetic perspective like Locked Up or Gangland.

The popular media is partially responsible for its love/hate relationship between street gangs and the masses by sensationalizing events or embracing certain gang figures who possess charismatic prestige, which leads to the dubious association between gangs and the citizenry. A major part of the population is interested in journalism or mediums of communication that revolve around scandal, gossip, and conflict, therefore, any news reporting which investigates street gang organizations is usually embraced because it will almost always contain those elements.

Popular mediums of communication should provide information that is essential, interesting, and necessary, but because the market dictates the outcome of news stories, it provides the citizenry with scandal, gossip, and conflict that helps create a pseudo-environment which over stimulates our central nervous system. What results is the contribution of the popular/underground media to the dumbing down of the society, and the decadence of post-modern culture by attacking the central nervous system. The central nervous system then mutates actions/reactions of people living amongst street gang organizations, which in turn helps reinforce the propagandist ideology.

CHAPTER 9: INTEREST GROUPS

All interests groups seek to influence government decision-making by pressuring legislators to pass policies that are beneficial to them. Most interest groups are non-government groups or independent associations with common interests, and many are non-profit organizations which have the public and the consumer's interests in mind.

Usually, interest groups are social/cultural groups, whose primary goal is not commercial, they maintain a consultative status with government organizations, and they use lobbying as their primary technique to influence government decision-makers. In order to influence legislators, lobbyists need access and connections, which usually includes an informal 'wine and dine' session, or simply establishing rapport or friendships with legislators to help influence decisions based on loyalty and empathy.

In the subterranean street culture, there are a few interest groups that lobby street gang legislators to pass policies on their behalf such as: party crews, tagging crews, non-profit organizations, drug dealers/narco-traffickers, organized criminals, and sometimes even law enforcement authorities.

Party crews are social groups whose primary concern is debauchery, partying, and fraternity, that sometimes seek to influence street gang legislators because they often loiter in gang-infested territory and

103

sometimes seek access to government conventions or festivals. Tagging crews are social groups whose primary concern is urban artwork and graffiti, that also seek to influence street legislators because they compete for wall space, which sometimes results in serious repercussions for tagging crews.

Traditional non-profit organizations include: 'Homies United' and 'Victory Outreach,' whose primary concern is to rehabilitate individual gang members or help them escape urban/prison politics to resume a civilian lifestyle.

Drug dealers/narco-traffickers are independent of street gang urban politics, but engage in commerce in inner cities and lobby street gang legislators for sovereignty and commercial markets. Organized criminals that often need commercial markets, territory, or protection at the street level often create loose coalitions with street gangs in order to maintain power and establish business practices.

Lastly, law enforcement agencies are special interest groups because they sometimes play a significant role in the prevention or eradication of street gang organizations, which sometimes results in corruption or scandal due to their involvement within street gang politics. Law enforcement agencies seek to influence street legislators through intimidation and prevention; however, coercion and blackmail are often lobbying techniques employed.

Throughout different regional blocs of the County of Los Angeles, many party crews developed in the early 90's in order to maintain fraternity, prestige, and reputation amongst their peers, but avoided joining a social contract because of the violence or pressure of gangs. Some of these party crews were sometimes associated with a certain street gang organization because of their geographical location.

Party crews originated as groups of like-minded individuals and friends who had a common interest in partying as their objective, but sometimes they needed protection from street gangs or other party crews. Sometimes they adopted pseudonyms like those of gang members, they emphasized a certain dress code with expensive clothing and style, they drove luxury vehicles, and they maintained a popular reputation amongst women.

Party crews feuded amongst each other because of territory, women, reputation, and association, which became similar to the street gang social contract. As party crews increased in size and reputation, street gangs began to perceive them as potential members with promising careers, thus they began putting pressure on these party crew associations.

Many party crews reacted with lobbying efforts to prevent gangs from passing policies which targeted their members as enemies. Street gangs relied on fear and intimidation in order to implement policy, and because they often viewed party crews as weak associations, they sometimes imposed intimidation practices or pressured them to join their gang. Some party crew members maintained close relations with decision-makers for utilitarian purposes; they established connections with influential gang members in order to allow them sovereignty without fear of repercussions, thereby avoiding a coercive draft.

Furthermore, during the Westside Renaissance of the Westside regional bloc, many party crews were extremely generous with their lobbying techniques because of the prestige and reputation of the festivals, thus seeking access to those cultural events. However, lobbying techniques were not always successful and thus sometimes resulted in extreme violence against the party crew association. When party crew members were drafted into a street gang, they usually brought their socialization of the party crew association with them and inadvertently helped transform the overall ideology of the organizational culture of their political party or the street gang, and thus become agents of change.

Party crews were originally meant to party and establish fraternity; however, they sometimes had conflicts with the gangs and began feuding, so they joined or merged to avoid a further conflict of interest which was beyond their element. Therefore, party crews were and sometimes still are considered interest groups because of their association and involvement with street gang organizations, and their utilization of lobbying techniques to influence decision-makers.

In the late '80's and early '90's, the tagging/graffiti phenomenon took the Los Angeles County by storm. Most taggers were associated with a crew; tagging crews were emerging from thin air and dominating the street subculture, which was threatening to street gang organizations. The main objective of a tagger was to gain street recognition by defacing public/private property continuously, and to join a crew that had a notorious reputation.

These individuals were known for tagging their aliases and crews on any kind of infrastructure or landmark, for vandalizing buses, and they were

106

consistently engaged in battles with other tagging crews. It was commonplace activity for taggers from opposite crews to gather around bus stops and take turns vandalizing a bus to see who was the most daring, who had the most style, and who had the most members willing to risk their freedom for the sake of the battle or the tagging crew association.

Tagging crews were social groups with a common interest of street recognition for their urban artwork; however, their subculture activity often conflicted with that of street gang organizations. Therefore, tagging crew associations became special interest groups who aimed for a utilitarian framework for their members. Many street gang members were known to intimidate graffiti writers because of their subordinate status within subterranean street culture, however, many tagging crews and specific individuals within that community had fierce reputations that were not to be trudged on lightly.

Tagging crews already had a subversive stigma because of their lack of respect for private/public property, but they also had other criminal elements attached to them such as: stealing, experimenting with and selling drugs, carrying illegal firearms, and occasionally engaging in physical violence against opposite crews. This resulted in certain graffiti writers and tagging crews becoming politicized by the street gang organization philosophy, which in turn, they started behaving or dressing more like street gang members.

Several graffiti writers and tagging crews actually joined a street gang organization, but maintained a dual sovereignty with the street gang and their tagging crew.

However, many tagging crew associations merged within a street gang or transformed their crew into an actual gang. It should be noted that a crucial distinct element that differentiates street gang from tagging crew philosophy is that most tagging crews are multicultural groups that champion diversity, while street gang organizations keep their diversity to a minimum.

During all the bustle of tagging crew sovereignty and graffiti writers becoming politicized, which in turn coined the term 'tag bangers', there were a lot of lobbying efforts on behalf of tagging crews towards street gangs. Individual graffiti writers and tagging crews would lobby street gang legislators to allow for their sovereignty to protect them against other gangs or opposing tagging crews, and provide illegal firearms or drugs. These lobbying techniques in the past were usually successful for a variety of reasons, however, a county-wide policy implemented during the 'Treaty of the South Side' of 1993-1994 by the Southernists imposed a green-light on tagging crews and enforced a draft. The draft ultimately reversed lobbying techniques that had previously been successful.

Not all tagging crews were affected by this policy though; many tagging crews joined the gangs voluntarily. Similar to party crews, tagging crew associations who joined a street gang brought their tagging crew socialization with them and helped transform the overall ideology and played a significant role as change agents to the overall culture of street gang organizations.

Party crews and tagging associations are not that common today; however, if they begin developing sporadically, Southernist policies will usually neutralize their efforts to maintain sovereignty within street gang territory. In street culture, special interests groups also play a secondary role as in popular government; however, when examining drug dealers, narco-traffickers, and organized criminals, it is clear that the need for a loose coalition is optimally required.

Drug dealers operate and coexist with street gangs in inner cities; however, they also operate in middle-class suburbs and sell drugs to more affluent consumers. The difference between the suburban drug dealer and the inner city dealer, (if the dealer is not from a street gang) is that those in the inner city must succumb to taxation without representation amongst street gangs.

Many drug dealers operating in inner cities share the same customer base, and often have street gang members as part of that commerce. Often, drug dealers or organized criminals maintain clandestine expertise in areas of communications, marketing, banking, transportation, and other negotiations throughout other states or countries, which gang members seek access to their availability of resources to keep their administration afloat.

Drug dealers and organized criminals usually possess capital and lines of communication or transportation, while street gangs possess followers, discipline, and organization. Drug dealers are special interest groups, whose primary objective is commercial gain, while most street gangs are primarily turf-oriented. They transcend state and international borders, but they use lobbying techniques when dealing within street gang boundaries.

Many drug dealers or organized criminals involve their entire families in the operation; therefore, a main concern for the drug dealer is overall protection and well-being. Because there is a fear of intimidation and fear of getting robbed by street gang members, drug dealers lobby street gang legislators for protection and sovereignty. Some of these drug dealers are allowed sovereignty; however, many do have to pay taxes on their revenues and do business with street gangs within those boundaries. Lobbying techniques on behalf of drug dealers are ambiguous because they sometimes obtain protection and sovereignty, but they sometimes get robbed, threatened, and physically harmed by gang members.

Drug dealers and organized criminals lobby urban politicians to pass policies that are beneficial to them and contribute monies to their campaigns to procure adequate representation. The relationship between the drug dealers and street gangs is one of necessity and reciprocity because they both rely on each other for survival; however, street gang legislators sometimes make secret deals with drug dealers behind closed doors and avoid accountability and transparency to the general public and their constituencies.

The goal of a street gang is to establish loose coalitions with drug/narco traffickers and organized criminals in order to provide protection to their assets within the boundaries of their territory, in exchange for commercial gain. Street gang organizations can provide different types of talents including: extortion, intimidation, or murder, while the drug/narco dealers or organized criminals can provide logistical land communications and support, as well as capital in commercial markets.

This loose coalition of extensive resources can facilitate the bribing of real government officials, intimidate or extort those who cannot be bribed, and perhaps murder those that try to impede the goals of their commercial markets, typical of many type of business practices and interest groups. If this type of loose coalition functions smoothly, it is highly possible to generate a more efficient and effective organization due to the lack of bureaucratic red tape that many government organizations maintain.

Non-profit organizations including; Homies United and Victory Outreach, are non-government organizations which help victims and victimizers of street gang violence escape a life of criminal propagandist ideology which is becoming a serious threat to national security. These non-profit organizations are extremely concerned with domestic and regional instability, as well as international concerns leading to state failure, like in certain Central American countries. Victory Outreach is a community-based church organization that helps lost and troubled people find their way to a religious belief system, specifically in inner cities plagued by gang violence.

Although Victory Outreach is a highly recognized international organization, it has a very significant presence around the Los Angeles County because of its successful effort in the rehabilitation of street gang members. Since the '60's, it has played the role of a special interest group to street gang organizations because of its lobbying efforts to end gang violence. Because of the separation of church and state within street gangs, it does not have as much overall influence; however, individuals are drawn in on a personal level when salvation seems to have more sovereignty than their street gang organization.

Throughout the Los Angeles County, Victory Outreach utilizes the liberal arts including: music, poetry, literature, film, and theatre, to capture an audience that has been socialized by street gang philosophy and sees the dramatization of it in the arts as a way to elude it. Many high-ranking Southernist officials, and also street-level criminal urban politicians have renounced their involvement in street gang and prison politics to give their lives to religion as a path to salvation, forgiveness, and repentance.

Victory Outreach helps to facilitate the transition from street gang hoodlum to law-abiding citizen, therefore, the non-profit organization lobbies street gang politicians to not seek personal vendettas on those who have found a higher meaning in life, but encourages more soldiers to go on missions for Christ, specifically in the City of Lost Angels where many troubled individuals seem to need guidance.

In 1996, a non-government outreach organization in El Salvador began the process of dealing with an overwhelming gang epidemic which had plagued the nation. Throughout the 90's, the United States began dealing with an overcrowded prison population, and saw the deportation of illegal criminal immigrants as an alternative solution. Most of those illegal criminal immigrants were engaged in street gangs throughout the Los Angeles County, but were born in Mexico, Honduras, Guatemala, Nicaragua, and El Salvador. Coincidentally, when these illegal criminals were

112

imprisoned for street gang activity, they were also deported to their countries of origin, even though they had been completely socialized in the United States.

This led to the widespread activity of street gang organizations in the Central American region and led to its proliferation abroad. Homies United began as a proactive organization to deal with this epidemic that had swept through the region, specifically with the notorious MS 13, the Mara Salvatrucha. MS is known as a ruthless street gang that has its roots in Los Angeles, and began exporting its code of honor and existence throughout Central America and various major cities throughout the United States, which was directly caused by the deportation of illegal criminals.

Homies United was an organization created by ex-gang members who wanted to deal with street gang defectors that no longer wanted to uphold the social contract, but needed protection because they feared repercussions from their former street gang organization. Homies United opened a Los Angeles chapter two years after its origin in El Salvador, and has since lobbied street gang politicians to eradicate gang violence, to allow defectors to walk away peacefully without reprisals, and to join grassroots struggles in political activism against police brutality, misconduct, or racism.

However, many high-level officers within the organization have been arrested for numerous crimes including: murder, conspiracy to commit murder, extortion, drug dealing, and so forth. During the Rampart Scandal of the LAPD, Homies United and other street gang members were involved in the National Day of Protest to Stop Police Brutality

Campaign, and found themselves aligned with other political activists.

Their main concern was an international one; that Los Angeles-based street gang organizations were and continue to help facilitate state failure in Central America, which also leads to a political act of war, not a simple, street gang regional law-enforcement problem.

Many of those ex-gang member activists marched to the LAPD headquarters and protested against police brutality, which many gang members had direct connections with, and were extremely open with accusations. Because of their exposure of police brutality, racism, and misconduct, LAPD officer's targeted Homies United officials and other gang members within the area, however, it wasn't long before the LAPD's Rampart Scandal attracted international attention, and was involved in federal civil rights lawsuits and corruption scandals.

Most gang members perceive police officers as gangsters with badges because their conduct towards them goes beyond the law and often involves corruption, misconduct, coercion, or blackmail. Sometimes police officers are considered special interest groups because they also use lobbying techniques when dealing with street gangs that include prevention and commerce, but sometimes lead to corruptibility.

In 2002, the L.A. Weekly published an article that outlined the history of LAPD scandals which included:

1902-1905, corruption scandals force five LAPD police chiefs to retire.

1922-1923, more than one-hundred police officers discharged for police brutality.

1926—LAPD declares war against organized crime and bootleg gangsters; philosophy is "wanted dead or alive."

1936—Following the invasion of depression refugees, police chief usurps state power and imposes a "bum blockade" against migrant workers.

1943—Sailors from Chavez Ravine Navel Base riot against Mexican-American teenagers and LAPD arrests victims, which is then followed by the Zoot Suit riots.

1951—Event known as Bloody Christmas because of the bloody brutality seven Latinos received while in police custody.

1965—Watts riots sparked by controversial arrests.

1975-1982, fifteen people die from being subdued by notorious police chokeholds.

1982—LAPD increases anti-gang units after African-American gang members begin to proliferate.

1988—Mass gang sweeps throughout Los Angeles county including Hispanic/Black gang members who are given jail time for practically anything.

1992—Race riots followed by Rodney King beating and acquittal of four police officers.

1998—Rampart scandal, where C.R.A.S.H. officer, Rafael Perez, is arrested for stealing six pounds of cocaine and implicates seventy officers in police corruption and misconduct.

In retrospect, the 1992 Los Angeles race riots were triggered by judicial injustice and police brutality. After one Hispanic and three Caucasian police officers were acquitted by an all-white jury for beating an unarmed incoherent motorist, which was videotaped by an objective onlooker, disillusioned inner city proletariats began rioting in the streets of Los Angeles. Racial profiling and police brutality had reached a climax, thus the verdict of the trial sparked a collective opportunity for mostly low-income Blacks and Hispanics to engage in mass law-breaking including looting, arson, and random shootings.

Within hours, the streets of South Central Los Angeles turned into a battle zone as proletariat looters and snipers shot at police officers, rescue workers, media/police helicopters, and Korean shopkeepers with assault weapons they had looted from surplus stores.

Multiracial rioters used Molotov cocktails to torch motorcars, block intersections, and systematically burn capitalist enterprises and government buildings, which forced law enforcement agencies to withdraw from the battle zone. Mass looting and rioting spread to other locations around the Los Angeles County, which forced state officials to declare a curfew, send in federal military troops and set up a barracks at police stations and other focal points of interest or targets for rioters, in the middle of urban neighborhoods.

Many viewed the Los Angeles riots as opportunist anarchy used for personal benefit because many luxury goods had been looted, however, it was also a period of social unrest where proletariats joined forces and focused on the common enemy, which included law enforcement, the market economy, and the bourgeoisie.

Many street gang organizations were heavily involved in the 1992 Los Angeles riots; however, many of them used it as an opportunity to settle scores with hostile enemies and police officers. Those individuals who made up the counterculture, had enough collective influence and disillusionment to bring the city of Los Angeles to a standstill, and helped trigger collective spontaneous rioting in other cities including: San Francisco, San Jose, Las Vegas, Tampa, Seattle, Atlanta, New York City, Oakland, Chicago, Phoenix, and Madison.

In 1998, C.R.A.S.H. officer; Rafael Perez, was arrested for stealing six pounds of cocaine from an LAPD evidence room. C.R.A.S.H. (Community Resources against Street Hoodlums) was an elite anti-gang unit created by the LAPD to suppress gang activity and gather intelligence on street gang organizations. In order to infiltrate these organizations, C.R.A.S.H. officers had to know everything about street gangs. For example, they collected intelligence on: history, origin, the shot-callers, pseudonyms, girlfriend's or mother's houses, what cars they drove, what tattoos they had, and any other intelligence which could be of possible use.

In many ways, those police officers had to socialize with gang members, understand the neighborhood mentality, and adopt their thought process to anticipate the subsequent moves of gang members. This is what led C.R.A.S.H. units to have a stigma attached to them as a police gang, specifically in the Rampart Division because they had "their own way of doing things," which was cutting corners, being unsupervised, and exercising their own jurisprudence.

C.R.A.S.H. officers had a logo, plaques, matching tattoos; they wore patches on jackets, and were also rewarded or recognized for having hits and killings, similar to gang members having stripes for shootings and murders. After Rafael Perez was arrested, he exposed and implicated at least seventy other police officers in patterns of misconduct including; brutal beatings, bad shootings, routine lying, writing false reports, planting drugs and guns on gang members, and selling drugs. This was known as the Rampart Scandal, and was also associated with the arrest of police officer David Mack for a bank robbery, who was a good friend of Rafael Perez, and who was a possible suspect in the killing of rapper Biggie Smalls.

David Mack and Rafael Perez had been known to work security for the Death Row record label, which had strong ties with a blood street gang from Compton, and were also seen in numerous pictures throwing up gang signs and dressing all in red. C.R.A.S.H. officers in Mar Vista were also known for their pattern of misconduct, and in 1994 the unit received another blow to its public image for locking up two Culver City 13 gang members in a holding tank with rival enemies—Venice Shoreline Crips, which were subsequently beaten for hours without police intervention.

Other patterns of police misconduct include: regional injunctions that are usually challenged by civil rights organizations, routine beatings for disobedience and lack of cooperation, dropping off gang members in rival neighborhoods, drinking on the job, confiscating drugs/monies/weapons without arresting perpetrators, planting evidence, implementing physical damage to cars, locking car keys inside of gang member's trunk, blackmail, and a laundry list of other activities.

Throughout the Los Angeles County, police officers who patrol gang territories are often known for their misconduct and jurisprudence which most gang members can relate to. The events in Rampart and other areas in the Los Angeles County are precedent examples that question the legitimacy of street patrol units that abuse their authority and violate civil rights. Corrupt police officers are often responsible for lengthy prison terms of gang members because many individuals do not have enough resources to protect themselves from the judicial system that offers them plea bargains versus life sentences.

All street gang organizations consider law enforcement agencies real and natural enemies, thus police officers have often been targets of violence because of their conduct towards those in the subculture. When police officers are gunned down in the line of duty, they sometimes retaliate and come

119

down hard on the street gang that has assumed responsibility for the murder, thus many times they have arrested suspects for crimes that result in harsh prison sentences.

The history of the Los Angeles Police Department demonstrates how many public officials in law enforcement are easily corruptible. Street gang organizations, drug/narco traffickers, and organized criminals can often view law enforcement organizations as special interest groups simply by allowing a flow of capital to infiltrate specific police units.

As a loose coalition is developed in specific communities, law enforcement authorities can be weakened, thus observation of such phenomena is assumed as a weak deterrent to regional instability. This loose coalition can be an effective tool to indirectly weaken the regime of law enforcement, therefore, with an effective and efficient street-level criminal operation, police officials can be considered interest groups who must lobby street gang public officials for information-swapping and certain levels of access to criminal markets. In many instances, police officials service that loose coalition.

CHAPTER 10: INTERNATIONAL RELATIONS

After nation-states have exploited their domestic resources and a battle for scarcity, power, and wealth develops, they begin to move beyond their territory to accumulate land, capital, and labor. The struggle for regional power means that nation-states must make preparations for defense and build up their military capabilities to extend their sphere of influence throughout the region. Through the use of force, intimidation, and propaganda skills, nation-states strive for power, national security, and domination, thus usually resulting in a regional hegemony, where one state has influence over other states' foreign/domestic affairs.

The regional hegemon uses its military capabilities to influence the international community and begins annexing resources, land, setting up commonwealths and colonies, engaging in foreign direct investment to increase their gross national product (GNP), and finding innovative ways to influence states to pass policies that are beneficial to them. Social contracts were created because the state of nature is anarchic and a balance of power is necessary, however, in the international community, the atmosphere is much more anarchic because it is a macrocosmic perception, and nation-states do not want to be dominated by a regional hegemon that tries to undermine their sovereignty.

During the middle of the twentieth century, the international community started moving into a global village where information and technology became more important for wealth and domination rather than land and labor, therefore, creating virtual states that are more cost-efficient and can produce goods and services overseas and sell them on the foreign market. Virtual states invest in human resources, technology, and information, and compete for power and national security on the international stage; therefore, the new struggle for power does not necessarily involve armed conflict.

The world is divided between three different ideologies of international political economy, including liberalism, mercantilism/nationalism, and Marxism.

Liberalism maintains that politics and economics are two separate spheres of influence that are not dependent on each other and that economic policy should be dictated by the free market. In order to maximize efficiency, establish economic thrift, and maintain individual welfare, a market economy develops spontaneously based on the principles of supply and demand. Individuals create and facilitate markets for trade and exchange to satisfy consumer needs, and naturally increase the range of goods and services so that both parties in the exchange benefit, and trade goods and services voluntarily.

The basic concept of liberalism and the market economy is to improve their well-being in the scheme of things, therefore rationalizing a cost/benefit analysis in regards to goods and services and maintaining economic growth.

Mercantilism/nationalism maintains that economic growth and activity are subordinate to the objective or goals of the nation-state, which can range anywhere from having a peaceful, neutral state without a military, to a totalitarian fascist regime. Mercantilists believe that the sovereignty of the state is dependent on the wealth of the nation and its power, therefore economic resources and policies are necessary for national security and development. Economic and political decisions are made simultaneously because they are dependent on each other for the same goal of wealth and power; however, the interests of the nation-state are primary.

Some political analysts use a four-point approach to describe this. 1. Wealth is an absolutely essential means to power, whether for security or for aggression. 2. Power is essential or valuable as a means to the acquisition or retention of wealth. 3. Wealth and power are each proper ultimate ends of national policy. 4. There is long-run harmony between these means, although in particular circumstances it may be necessary for a time to make economic sacrifices in the interests of military security and therefore also of long-run prosperity.

In regards to the international community, mercantilists believe that self-sufficiency is necessary for wealth and power even though the benefits are disproportionate to other nation-states.

Marxism developed as a reaction to capitalism and the market economy because the means of production that are privately owned exploit wage labor, thus transforming labor into a dispossessed commodity that can be traded and exchanged as goods and services. Marxism criticizes capitalism and maintains that its demise is inevitable because of three economic laws which are: disproportionality, which is that capitalism tends to overproduce products, goods, and services that consumers cannot afford and causes periods of instability in the market economy.

Secondly, that capitalism is governed by fierce competition and profit that forces the accumulation of wealth in the hands of the bourgeoisie (middle-class), and forces the exploitation of the working class proletariats. Lastly, that the falling rate of profit, which decreases the incentive to invest, save, and accumulate, increases unemployment levels and leads to economic stagnation and poverty. Marxism believes that the impoverished proletariat will rise up and overthrow the bourgeoisie with a social revolution and replace the economic system with a socialist agenda.

In the late '80's, the street gang organization of Lennox 13 began its efforts at expansion with a move to the Downtown/Central Los Angeles regional bloc in the Hollywood area. Street gang areas usually have a high-density level that saturates the market economy, thus individuals from the Lennox 13 street gang began relocating to the Hollywood area to extend their sphere of influence and exploit available resources.

Often, individual gang members are in hiding and running from law enforcement, so they end up in open and sometimes hostile territories, but they take their lifestyle with them. The Lennox 13 street gang started a commonwealth in the Northeast regional bloc called the 'Hollywood Bandits' and began recruiting impressionable youths and known comrades, and they began expanding their network of trade through colonial influence.

As a small colony with a fatherland in a different regional bloc, the Hollywood Bandits had to deal with open hostility from other established gangs within the area including: 18th St, Mara Salvatrucha, Armenian Power, The Magician's Cub, and other well-known street gangs within the region.

With assistance and resources from Lennox headquarters, the Hollywood Bandits were able to establish a tight-knit commonwealth that engaged in racketeering, extortion, murder, and drug commerce, however, because of their illegal activities and pressure from law enforcement, they would relocate like wandering vagabonds to North Hollywood, Eagle Rock, Highland Park, and Anaheim.

In general, many gang members are forced into exile by law enforcement because they are wanted for criminal activities, and they relocate to areas where family, friends, relatives, or other networks are in place, thus they take their lifestyle with them and reinforce the propagandist ideology of Los Angeles street gangs. For example, many Southernists migrated to Las Vegas, Nevada in the early '90's because it was wide open for drug trafficking and street gang organizations were not well established.

Many Lennox 13 gang members migrated to Las Vegas as well because of forced exile, labor, or other reasons, while simultaneously establishing networks with other migrant Southernists. The struggle for power and wealth develops in any area where market economies develop to provide an availability of resources based on the principles of supply and demand, especially when the protagonists establish a mercantilist agenda. In Las Vegas, local residents developed their own street gang organizations to resist the outside influence that the migrants brought with them; therefore, the Southernists established networks and loose coalitions to build up their defense and national security.

Some Lennox 13 gang members also relocated to Denver, Colorado to establish a commonwealth which also reinforced the propagandist ideology there, and began colonizing and socializing local residents who lived in rundown communities and public housing units. In general, Los Angeles has an aura of being affluent and glamorous, thus even street gang members are looked at with mysticism and reverence because of their international public image, which intrigues those who are easily influenced because they want to be part of the organizational culture, even though they have never been to Los Angeles.

Lennox 13 gang members made several attempts to establish commonwealths in Hollywood, Las Vegas, Phoenix, Denver, and Tijuana, and expand their sphere of influence throughout different territories, yet neither was as successful as in Albuquerque, New Mexico, where they accumulated more land, capital, and labor than in their own fatherland.

In the early '90's, a group of explorers from Lennox 13 traveled to Albuquerque, New Mexico, and discovered a poverty-stricken wasteland that had potential for increased gross national product (GNP). There were many low-income residents, who had substance abuse problems, but there was not much availability of drug resources and the demand was higher than the supply. The Lennox 13 gang members quickly took advantage of the situation and asked the fatherland to send drugs and monies to set up a commonwealth where their profit margin could increase more than one-hundred percent. They quickly began accumulating land, capital, labor, and extended their sphere of influence throughout the region and used their communication and propaganda skills for fear and intimidation.

As they engaged in foreign direct investment and increased human resources in the form of recruitment and expansion, a struggle for power and wealth developed with competitive rivals, who were predominantly from a Black Crips street gang from Los Angeles, the Rolling 60's. Most street gang organizations from the Los Angeles County are mercantilists because the goals and objectives of state growth, development, and representation are primary to commerce, however, they do recognize that power is parallel to wealth and they adopt economic and political policies simultaneously for the sovereignty of the state.

The Lennox 13 gang members, along with other Southernists from other neighborhoods who also migrated to the area, began preparing for urban warfare by building up their military defense to eliminate healthy competition and create a monopoly in the market. The low-intensity conflict took a turn when the Rolling 60's murdered a Southernist from the Temple Street gang, which the conflict turned into a street war that left the Southernists victorious with limited competition. Southernist shot-callers in

Albuquerque were subsidizing individuals who would murder any rival from Rolling 60's and other opposition, thus law enforcement agencies began investigative surveillance into the operation.

As the Lennox 13 gang members and other Southernists established power, national security, and domination, an unforeseen event that involved child abuse led investigators to raid known drug houses. One of the first perpetrators to get arrested from Lennox 13, Shaggy from the Tokers, cooperated with law enforcement agencies, and then joined the witness protection program. The perpetrator snitched on countless fellow gang members, which resulted in the downfall of the Albuquerque commonwealth.

Many were arrested for racketeering, extortion, murder, attempted murder, drug trafficking, some received consecutive life sentences while others received the death penalty. The trial received international attention and the Lennox 13 gang members adopted a new reverence and reputation amongst the prison congress and with the Southernists because of their attempts at imperialism.

During the late 1980's, a wave of immigrants from El Salvador were seeking political refuge in the United States because of a bloody civil war that divided their country. As the children of those immigrants grew up into young adults, the need to create a social contract as a means of protection from street gangs and other pressure groups seemed imperative.

Most of the Salvadoran immigrants settled in Washington D.C. and Los Angeles, California, in the Downtown/Central Los Angeles regional bloc throughout the Hollywood area where gang activity was running rampant. Throughout the Pico Union district, the 18th Street gang controlled the community by intimidating citizens and keeping them in fear, therefore, many Central American immigrants in the area joined the gang voluntarily while some were coaxed.

A group of Salvadoran immigrants created their own street gang organization known as Mara Salvatrucha or MS, to resist other street gangs and maintain their sovereignty in a foreign environment. Many of them had been guerilla fighters in their home towns and were no strangers to extreme violence, so creating a street gang organization and struggling for power, wealth, and national security seemed like a walk in the park.

Many of them had lost their sense of fear, they were not afraid of urban warfare because they had been exposed to: police torture, incarceration in a third world country, hardcore criminal activity, military and guerilla fighting, and living on the streets; so, gang culture helped provide fraternity that was non-existent. As their socialization within street gang culture increased, they incorporated loathsome methods of torture and murder they had experienced in their home towns to the urban warfare existing in the Los Angeles County.

In the early 1990's, the United States government passed an immigration policy that exported gang members who were arrested for criminal activity to their home countries because of increased gang violence and lack of prison space. Some hardly spoke Spanish and were now foreigners in their own land, yet they began forming networks with teenagers and young adults who were abandoned, unemployed, and alienated, thus they began exporting the propagandist ideology of Los Angeles street gang culture. Throughout the Central American region, deported gang members spread the street lifestyle, they enlisted eager recruits, and they easily impressed local residents who coveted living in the United States, specifically in Los Angeles, California.

As street gang violence and gang membership increased throughout the Americas, authorities in Guatemala and El Salvador began building and designating prisons specifically for gang members because of the lack of social infrastructure, resources, and monies, to effectively deal with this sweeping phenomenon. These new street gang organizations in Central America went beyond personal and collective street violence and extended their criminal activities to: kidnapping, car smuggling, credit card fraud, bank robbery, property expropriation, assassinations, institutional corruption, criminal anarchy, and people smuggling, which began the first wave of street gang refugee flows.

Most of the deported immigrants were from 18th Street and MS, and through default, the United States federal government has now helped the globalization of street gang organizations, which have now become a regional hegemony throughout Central America.

The geopolitics of MS and 18th Street have transcended national borders and the deported gang members could be considered displaced personnel or expatriates of street gang organizations from the Los Angeles County, therefore, they are inadvertently sent to live abroad, look for commercial and criminal

130

opportunities, study foreign languages and cultures, and in essence obtain international education and training. MS and 18th Street have taken their territorial rivalry from Los Angeles to the Americas; they identify themselves with extreme tattooing of the face, they build international networks through the internet, telecommunications, and other mediums of communication, and are in essence creating a virtual state where much of their influence, power, and wealth, can be obtained from abroad.

Government corruption in Central America plays a significant role in allowing street gangs and organized criminals to operate with impunity through various territories and borders by blurring the traditional lines between criminal and political violence, which in turn creates a political agenda for criminal organizations that can help create a narco-state.

Some of these street gang organizations have moved from a loose to a powerful coalition with organized criminals and drug traffickers, former military and police personnel, intelligence and security officers, all of who have helped establish a narco-state through a highly profitable criminal cartel. The main objective is to ensure a failing state in order to allow mobility in commercial markets.

Most of the deported gang members have an objective to return to the United States, specifically to the gang Mecca of Los Angeles, however, because of the harsh crackdowns and pressure from law enforcement agencies, when they return to the country illegally they migrate to the east coast or other parts of the country. These new globalized street gang organizations are more organized and assist fellow gang members with protection, housing, refuge, and commercial/criminal opportunities to facilitate their transitions back or newly arrived into the United States. Law enforcement agencies have found MS and 18th Street gang members throughout numerous states within the union.

The Immigration and Customs Enforcement Agency (ICE), which is part of the Department of Homeland Security, rounds up foreign gang members as part of maintaining national security and gang enforcement, and works with law enforcement agencies in Honduras, Guatemala, El Salvador, Mexico, and throughout the states, to discuss techniques about how deportation efforts have not decreased gang membership, and how it has internationalized street gang organizations.

As mentioned before, MS and 18th Street have moved into other capital-intensive enterprises including human smuggling of undocumented immigrants, counterfeiting identifications, international arms trafficking, organized drug commerce, and have engaged in much more violent behavior including domestic/international executions and holding residents hostage. Authorities in Central America have adopted an anti-gang policy called *"Mano Dura,"* which is an extremely draconian policy that incarcerates individuals for having tattoos or belonging to a street gang, but it has been compared by civil rights advocates to the tortures and murders of the 80's during the civil wars of Central America.

Coincidentally, many prisoners have died because of guard negligence in El Salvador, including two separate prison fires in 18th St and MS cell blocks which left almost two-hundred prisoners dead. As recently as August 2005, in three separate Guatemalan prison riots between 18th Street and MS rivals, at least thirty-one inmates were murdered. Some inmates had weapons ranging from knives to assault weapons like AK 47's, and in many cases where inmates have died, investigations have concluded that prison guards and faculty were directly responsible. MS and 18th St have taken their low-intensity street rivalry into an international high-intensity conflict that transcends national borders, and both street gangs have helped export street gang phenomenon across the globe by increasingly reinforcing the propagandist ideology through international relations.

CHAPTER 11: THE TREATY OF THE SOUTH SIDE

In the summer of 1993, the Southernist senators of the prison congress decreed a general peace treaty agreement amongst all street gangs in Southern California, which resulted in a temporary deferral of urban warfare. The African-American Bloods and Crips gangs had declared a peace treaty in 1992 after the Los Angeles riots, and set the precedent for the Treaty of the South Side of Hispanic street gangs.

The general agreement had been debated and discussed by committees for several months, but once it was ratified it marked the end of an era for the historical context and development of street gang organizations. The chief architects of the general agreement had an economic agenda for the peace treaty and immediately took action to enforce its protocols.

The basic underlying principle of the treaty was that if any particular street gang undermined the authority of the agreement, repercussions would be suffered by their fellow gang members in prison or on the streets by collective action. This fundamental principle was known as the red light/green-light phenomenon, where a red light suggests peace and security, while a green-light suggests naked aggression by a multitude.

Once the underground media reported the information to the general public, urban street politicians had to hold several press conferences to discuss the basic principles of the peace treaty; meetings were held constantly for street gang/political reeducation. The basic principles of the treaty included: promoting peace, establishing security, and engaging in economic development, which the council members of each particular street gang organization had to convey and enforce amongst their general public and constituents.

According to the peace agenda, street gang organizations were not allowed to engage in urban warfare amongst each other, however, they were encouraged and allowed to declare war against Black street gangs, and if any battles materialized with other Hispanic gangs, they would have to report it immediately to their city council.

The security agreement maintained that street gang members could pass through as transients through other neighborhoods and not suffer repercussions or reprisals, but they had to pass through with the intent of establishing non-threatening relations. The agenda maintained that street gang organizations should engage in capital-intensive programs to build up a surplus and increase their GDP, to help pay a federal income tax to the senate as a form of taxation with representation throughout the prison system.

After a few weeks of political reeducation and assimilation of the general peace agreement, the Southernist senators held a meeting in the Elysian Park of East Los Angeles, the Elysian Park Conference, where street gang organizations from all over Southern

California attended to further discuss the principles of the general agreement. Throughout the conference, many rival street gang organizations were allowed to fight one-on-ones to settle scores and take out their aggression, although it was monitored by chief participants of the agreement, and it wasn't allowed to escalate further.

After the basic principles were conveyed to all street gangs in an all-inclusive manner, they broke off into sections according to regional bloc status, to discuss regional goals for achieving cooperation in solving social and economic concerns. It appeared like a scene from the motion picture 'The Warriors' where at least one thousand gang members from all over Southern California convened, including classic rivals standing next to each other, to acquiesce the basic principles of the general agreement.

During the conference, the park was surrounded by the LAPD in riot gear, patrol squad cars, helicopters, and officers on foot in case the conference resulted in anarchy; however, the Elysian Park Conference was a success for the general agreement and helped trigger the self-restraint and cooperation of street gang organizations.

The Treaty of the South Side was instrumental in reducing gang violence in Hispanic communities, however many began channeling their efforts into urban warfare against Black street gangs. Many Hispanic gangs did not have a significant Black street gang presence throughout their regional bloc or vicinity, so it facilitated their building up of military capabilities, capital-intensive programs, and GDP.

However, some gangs were at a disadvantage, including the ones in Compton and South Central where the Black street gangs flourished, which forced them to engage in inexorable, racial urban warfare, which resulted in heavy casualties.

In the Westside regional bloc, a meeting held at Imperial Beach, the Imperial Beach Conference, resulted in the cooperation of the Westside street gang organizations to promote peace, security, and economic development throughout the region. The basic principles and agenda of the general agreement, the regional goals, and the social/economic concerns were discussed among high-ranking public officials of the Westside regional bloc and Southernist senators.

Other issues included territorial adjustments such as small cliques or gangs being drafted into larger street gangs, the coercion and assault on party/tagging crew associations, and urban warfare against Black street gangs. Throughout the Westside, the general agreement threatened the sovereignty of small street gangs because the chief architects of the peace treaty did not want pockets of small gangs because of accountability, districting, and federal tax regulations, thus many were coerced into larger street gangs but some petitioned the decision and were officially recognized as a legitimate gang.

Other territorial adjustments included the drafting of tagging/party crew associations because of their volume, therefore many tagging/party crew members accepted the decision, some abandoned their attachment to the association, and some resisted the annexation and started their own street gang by petition.

During the Imperial Beach Conference, decision-makers concluded that Westside regional bloc street gangs would declare urban warfare on the Venice Shoreline Crips, an active Black street gang located in the unincorporated community of Venice. The urban warfare was ostensibly an ethnic cleansing because of the heavy casualties suffered by the Shoreline Crips, which were collectively attacked by the street gangs of Venice, Sotel, Culver City, and Santa Monica, however, the Shorelines retaliated with serious counterattacks that left the Westside in a state of emergency.

During a Westside meeting, the Lennox 13 gang was asked for assistance and participation in the street warfare against the Shorelines. But, as the Lennox gang organization pondered the distance and involvement, the Shorelines passed through the Lennox neighborhood one evening and caught some of the Lennox 13 gang members by surprise, showed their flag and weapons, but maintained a non-aggression pact with no intentions of warfare.

Moreover, this event became the determining factor for the Lennox gang to remain neutral because the Shorelines could have murdered a few of their popular gang members, thus they rejected the offer with justification and sincerity, but worked cooperatively to reach other goals. Although the urban warfare on the Westside increased the death and incarceration rate for gang members in the region, objective analysts were impressed by the regional cooperation of the Westside street gangs, which once had perennial rivalries.

Coincidentally, the Westside regional bloc worked cooperatively to enhance the region's image by promoting cultural festivals and mega-events to attract public support and tourism, specifically the Lennox, Venice, and the Culver City 13 gangs. Along the LAX Airport area, the street gang organization of Lennox declared urban warfare on small pockets of Black street gangs and drug dealers around their neighborhood, which was directly related to the murder of one of their popular and well-revered individuals by the Rolling 60's.

While Venice, Culver City, Sotel, and Santa Monica were engaged in urban warfare with the Venice Shoreline Crips, and the Lennox 13 gang was engaged in urban warfare with Rolling 60's and Eucalyptus Mob, the Inglewood 13 street gang organization, which was one of the main Hispanic street gangs within the Westside, did not make a significant effort to declare urban warfare against the significant presence of Black street gangs throughout the area including: Crenshaw Mafia, Swans Blood Gang, Inglewood Family, Queen Street Bloods, and Inglewood 111th.

As a result, the Inglewood 13 gang was denounced by the Westside regional bloc, and they became disassociated with the Westside street gang organizations during the cultural festivals and mega-events of the general peace treaty agreement. The general agreement also allowed for the intensification of drug commerce throughout the Westside because of increased networking, cooperation, and connections developed by the general agreement which helped contribute to the coalition of regional goals, which in turn neglected the principal of national self-determination.

As the general peace treaty agreement progressed and developed, Security Councils were developed in regional blocs to handle disputes that could threaten the peace accord. Security Councils could make recommendations to parties involved in conflicts, use diplomatic measures to resolve disagreements, and after all options had been exhausted and a danger still existed that could threaten regional peace, they could impose acts of aggression or take enforcement measures.

Temporary green-light public policy was implemented when issues could not be resolved through diplomacy, so rival street gangs used windows of opportunity to assume aggression. Security Councils also imposed the federal taxation for the maintenance and development of the county-wide peace agreement, which became a cumbersome regulation for some street gangs.

Throughout the East Los Angeles regional bloc, a group of rival factions known as the Maravilla gangs defected from the general peace treaty agreement, which was known as the Maravilla Tax Revolt, who then became known as green-light gangsters. A green-light street gang organization included any organization that went against the peace accord. Prior to the peace accord, the Maravilla gangs had perennial rivalries with each other; however, after the general peace agreement imposed federal tax regulations, they joined forces and orchestrated a strong united front against all street gang organizations and the prison congress. The Maravilla gangs included: Arizona Maravilla, El Hoyo Maravilla, Ford Maravilla, Fraser Maravilla, Gage Maravilla, High Times Maravilla,

Juarez Maravilla, Lote Maravilla, Lopez Maravilla, Lomita Maravilla, Marianna Maravilla, Project Boys Maravilla, and Rascals Maravilla. The Maravilla gangs criticized the senators and the peace treaty because of federal tax regulations, biased public policy including green-lights or acts of aggression, and undermining their sovereignty, thus they became a subversive united organization.

The prison congress imposed collective security action against the Maravilla gangs; however, it did not deter their subversive behavior, thus they abandoned their participation in the peace accord. As a result, the green-light policy was implemented in county jails throughout Southern California; they were separated from the general population and the gang module, but were held under protective custody.

However, the green-light policy was not implemented in California State prisons because most of the Maravilla inmates had been incarcerated prior to the general peace agreement, which resulted in a conflict of interest with their representatives on the outside. Throughout the Westside regional bloc, biased public policy resulted in temporary green-lights or windows of opportunity, however, some street gang organizations used the peace accord to enhance their image and become Olympic Cities amongst Southern California street gang culture.

CHAPTER 12: MEGA-EVENT CITIES

According to Greg Andranovich, PhD at California State University, Los Angeles, and the mega-event strategy, cities compete on the global stage for world attention, tourism, and publicity. In the United States, cities compete for monies and resources from the federal government and their state legislature, thus bidding to host the Olympics is a way to bring prestige to the host city, or compete with world-class cities around the globe. Mega-event cities attract positive attention through media stories surrounding economic development or the mega-event strategy, while creating a tourist bubble.

The tourist bubble phenomenon is used for city marketing by creating a tourist destination which generates local tax revenues, including redevelopment in downtown areas that promote the city's cultural events, creating sporting conventions or facilities, and stimulating local businesses and economic growth. In order to actualize the mega-event strategy, these cities rely on public/private partnerships through coalitional power to pursue mega-event strategies and goals to facilitate hosting a prestigious event with as little public controversy or intervention as possible.

Informal agreements between politicians and members of the business community play a significant, yet instrumental role in procuring the bid for the Olympics. This was the case in Los Angeles during the

1984 Olympics when politicians used corporate sponsorships to host the mega-event without using public financing. Along with pursuing a redevelopment agenda through economic development, many cities use the mega-event strategy as a way to redefine its image and transform people's perception of the city through a tourist bubble, which serves as a catalyst for urban change.

Greg Andranovich also maintains that there are external conditions that can have a significant impact on pursuing the mega-event strategy which include: natural disasters, international public affairs, terrorist threats, and other current events of the day, nevertheless, hosting a prestigious event like the Olympics is a way to pursue economic development agendas to create good opportunities for short/long-term tangible/intangible benefits.

In 1994, the Treaty of the South Side became an external condition that had a significant impact on the way some street gang organizations pursued a redevelopment and economic development agenda. The general peace agreement temporarily deterred urban warfare and promoted regional goals, therefore, some neighborhoods saw this as a window of opportunity to promote their street gang organization and capture county-wide positive attention. In the Westside regional bloc, the Culver City 13 street gang used this opportunity to promote the propagandist ideology, while exporting their unconventional lifestyle through various mediums of communication including the underground media.

Most street gang organizations in Southern California wore the traditional solid dress code/colors;

144

however, the Culver City 13 gang members wore red Cincinnati Red's hats, red bandanas, red shoe laces, and other red clothing articles which still represented the propagandist ideology, but with more flare, which enhanced their public image because of their unconventional approach. On the other hand, when entering the industrial prison complex, the Culver City 13 gang members wore the blue flag of the South Side to represent the division of the prison congress between Northern and Southern California.

Throughout the Westside regional bloc, the Culver City gang members maintained a positive perception because of their lyrical/journalist contributions through the underground media that used pragmatism and creativity. The Culver City 13 underground lyricists formed a partnership with the Sotel 13 street gang, which then began promoting the Westside as a place to fear and covet simultaneously, through underground lyrical journalism.

In the Westside, the street gang organizations of Culver City, Sotel, Santa Monica, and Venice began having cultural festivals known as 'Westside Parties' which promoted peace and security throughout the region, but also provided an open platform for lyrical journalists to demonstrate their capabilities. However, Lennox and Venice had already maintained a positive relationship and two lyricists, Youngster from Lennox and Sneaky from Venice, were recording lyrics together previous to that.

But as the underground media began spreading stories down the coast through the grapevine and the lyrical content reached the unincorporated community of Lennox, those who were part of the progressive movement saw a window of opportunity to promote their street gang and their cultural lifestyle.

Many of the Lennox 13 gang members from the left-wing who were part of the progressive movement had been socialized in tagging/party crew associations, thus they saw the intangible benefits that hosting a mega-event would bring to their community. The Lennox 13 gang had a negative stigma attached to it because of their small presence of low-income working-class immigrants; also because one of their underground lyricists had a heavy accent, hence they were sometimes denounced as a "wetback gang."

Some individuals from Lennox understood that hosting a cultural festival would help reinvent their public image through positive county-wide attention, thus they began making preparations to host such an event. They took it up with the city council for discussion and were granted permission, however, the only provision the city council imposed was that no public financing would be used, which subsequently the event coordinators would raise the monies based on their own efforts.

They would ultimately be responsible for location, financing, logistics, promotion, and operations, which meant that revenues would be tax-free and benefits would be intangible and long-term for the gang. The redevelopment agenda required the significant presence of the other street gang organizations from the Westside; however, the Lennox 13 gang had never been invited to a Westside Party because of the negative stigma attached to them.

The Westside regional bloc cultural festivals included members of Sotel, Venice, Santa Monica, and

Culver City, which at the time considered themselves the four corners of the Westside, and excluded other gangs for ideological reasons. The event coordinators from Lennox 13 spent a significant amount of time distributing publications and promoting their mega-event through the underground media, which also sent a few diplomats to the Mar Vista projects with the intent of establishing peaceful relations with the Culver City 13 gang by extending them an invitation to the festival.

Rapport was easily established at the projects; coincidentally the Culver City 13 gang members were hosting a mega-event on that same weekend, but on a different day, thus an agreement was reached to attend each other's cultural functions.

The Culver City 13 gang members used informal agreements with local residents and members of the business community to host their mega-event festival in the basketball gymnasium of the Mar Vista Gardens Housing Project. Subsequently, the Culver City gang played host to a prestigious event which rendered positive media recognition.

The Lennox gang sent a convoy to the event as a means of proactive protection, which resulted in over one hundred gang members "dressed to impress", while shattering the negative stigma attached to their organization. The Culver City and Lennox street gang organizations had the most significant presence at the event because of their public image, their amount of personnel, their median age range, and other demographic factors, which resulted in mutual reverence and admiration which continued throughout the Westside Renaissance.

The mega-event was preceded the following day by the cultural festival held in the unincorporated community of Lennox at a private home on Larch Avenue, which brought back the same group of people and marked the beginning of the cultural Westside Renaissance experienced in the region during the general peace agreement. The cultural festival was broken up by the Lennox Sheriff Department, who marched to the private location in riot gear from three different locations.

The Lennox Sheriff became overwhelmed by the significant amount of opposite street gangs in unison and celebration; it could prove to be a problem for their careers. Because of the positive media attention and lack of violence, the cultural festival weekend played a historical role in pursuing the mega-event strategy for the Lennox and Culver City gangs, which developed a love and hate relationship, but also enjoyed prestigious attention, tourism, and publicity; Lennox and Culver City, a marriage made in the projects.

As the positive publicity of the Westside spread throughout the underground media, a conservative entrepreneur from the Lennox street gang formed an informal partnership with Culver City 13 gang members and other members of the business community, thus they began pursuing the mega-event strategy using public/private coalitional power to promote regional competitive sport and cultural festivals.

Many Culver City boys played football in high school and organized regional sporting events with other Westside street gangs, which resulted in increased positive media attention for the region and world-class entertainment for those interested in street gang culture. Often times, the Lennox street gang would host a classic football game between the street gangs of Venice and Culver City, which rendered positive media attention because of their capabilities and perennial rivalry, which drew a large crowd from different regional blocs.

When the Culver City 13 gang members hosted sporting events in the Mar Vista Gardens Projects, they showed off their graffiti, which rendered admiration and altered perception because of its precision, style, and dimension, similar to Florencia 13 which was associated with social-economic status.

The informal regional partnership used coalitional power and available resources to promote Westside regional bloc events including festivals and football games through advertisements, word-of-mouth, and distribution of publications, which resulted in mega-event city status for the Lennox and Culver City street gang organizations. Weekends became an opportunity to create a tourist bubble to invent a romanticized image to provide visitors with a pseudo-environment of socio-economic status, fraternity, and subversive, street gang culture excitement.

Many locations where constituents of the mega-event cities convened became focal points of interest and tourist destinations for visitors who traveled from different regional blocs or counties who expressed interest in the lifestyles of the Westside regional bloc. In Culver City, the Mar Vista Gardens Housing Project became a tourist destination for several geographical reasons including: availability of space to host cultural festivals on a regular basis, adequate sporting facilities to host regional competitions, and plenty of unmonitored and unlit streets to engage in criminal activity and commerce.

In the unincorporated community of Lennox, Lennox Park became a tourist destination for after-hours events, Inglewood Avenue, which is the focal street in the neighborhood, became a tourist destination for females traveling abroad, Isis Park was known for its availability to host regional sport competitions, and several dead-end streets served as locations to engage in unconventional activities.

Throughout the unincorporated community of Lennox, the tourist bubble helped develop growth for local businesses including: Acosta's Tacos, which stayed open late to cater to the 'Westside Party' crowd, Daniel's Barber Shop, which catered to local constituents, and during the cultural renaissance, had an increase in growth due to the prestige brought by the mega-event city status, and Jim's Diner, which had been a local hang-out for Lennox 13 gang members for years, experienced a period of growth due to the tourist bubble phenomenon.

The cultural festivals throughout the Westside drew such a large crowd that the public/private partnership, which became an independent committee, assumed responsibility and leadership for the events and created 'One Way Productions,' to host the mega-events in empty warehouses from Santa Monica to Torrance. The Westside events also provided a platform for underground lyricists to exhibit their talent and capabilities amongst a multitude, thus validating their creative style and methodology.

Style of dress began transforming as well because gang members from the Westside adopted a somewhat preppy look which also contributed to the cultural renaissance, and helped influence gang members from other areas to transform their dress code to a less conspicuous and intimidating look.

As the cultural festivals developed and progressed, physical altercations or disagreements between different street gangs became more commonplace. Temporary green-light policies were imposed sporadically, which allowed rival gangs windows of opportunity to assume aggression. The Westside cultural festivals came to a climax at a Gardena warehouse where the street gang organizations of Lennox and Gardena were involved in a physical altercation which left individuals of both street gangs hospitalized with bullet wounds, which contributed to temporary urban warfare between Lennox and Gardena 13 that lasted for months and led to a few murders.

The Lennox and Culver City relationship had been so well-established, that when the physical altercation between Lennox and Gardena began, the Culver City members assisted the Lennox boys by driving one of their members who suffered a bullet wound to the hospital, which continued the reciprocity of admiration and reverence for one another, but only lasted for a few more years until it reached its climax.

The Lennox and Culver City street gangs were directly responsible for the cultural Westside Renaissance, as well as how the regional bloc flourished during the Treaty of the South Side. Hosting a mega-event on the same cultural festival weekend resulted in a friendly relationship based on admiration and reverence; however, the relationship was often compromised by personal conflict or ambiguity. At the beginning of the relationship, both street organizations entertained each other in their respective neighborhoods and hosted each other in different focal points that would later become target destinations during temporary conflicts.

As the regional bloc attracted positive media attention, the Lennox and Culver City street gangs spent a significant amount of time in each other's neighborhoods which was unprecedented in street gang history, but was directly related to their mega-event city status.

During the Westside Renaissance, it was commonplace for the Lennox 13 gang members to gather in the Mar Vista Gardens Housing Projects during "after-hours" and regional sporting activities, similarly the Culver City gang members would write Culver City and Lennox 13 on public/private surfaces or sometimes hold private parties in Lennox territory.

The relationship extended outside of the regional bloc and carried over to other popular street gang cultural activities including: dance clubs, cars shows, popular ethnic festivals, street cruising, bars, or long weekend holidays celebrated in Ensenada, Tijuana, and Rosarito, Mexico. When they would see each other at these types of events or activities, they would establish rapport, stay in close proximity to each other, resume their lifestyles, yet keep a watchful eye just in case trouble unraveled, thus 'having each other's' backs' if altercations broke out.

On one occasion that marked the depth of their relationship, the Lennox and Culver City gangs attended a car show in the Los Angeles Coliseum which attracted county-wide street gang organizations. During a musical performance by a Los Angeles-based rap group, street gangs and fans in the audience threw their hands in the air to applaud the performer's capabilities and efforts.

Collectively, the Culver City 13 gang members began waving their red bandanas and Cincinnati Reds hats in the air because of their patriotism and representation of their neighborhood. Other street gangs in the audience began plotting against the Culver City 13 gang members because their red apparel was associated with the *Norteños*, the prison gang association from Northern California who were directly responsible for the polarization of the prison congress.

Most of the street gang organizations within the audience denounced the Culver City 13 gang solely because of their choice of color representation, thus the majority of street gang members of numerous neighborhoods walked out of the stadium to wait for the Culver City gang members while they planned a conspiracy. The Culver City 13 gang members gestured at the Lennox 13 boys as a plea for solidarity, instantly both street gangs recognized the need for camaraderie and walked out in unison.

Outside of the stadium, they were surrounded by more than two hundred gang members from all over the Los Angeles County ready to embark into a battle zone; however, the conspirators were overwhelmed by the amount of personnel from the Lennox 13 and

Culver City 13 gangs, and their eagerness to engage in a physical altercation. Through diplomatic and uncompromising efforts, the Westside street gangs were able to uphold their patriotism and representation of the regional bloc, while maintaining their defiance against the status-quo.

Despite the affinity and rapport that was established between the Lennox and Culver City street gangs, personal conflicts of interest between individual gang members resulted in temporary battles which compromised their relationship. Personal conflicts involving women, drugs, pride, patriotism, and other miscellaneous reasons resulted in feuds that started between two individuals that forced the entire gang to follow suit reluctantly.

The love and hate relationship lasted for a few years until it reached its climax in 1997 at a private party in a Culver City bar, where a gathering of women, Culver City gang members, and Lennox gang members, resulted in absolute chaos. The night was progressing relatively smoothly, until a disagreement unfolded between a Culver City gang member, his girlfriend, and two Lennox gang members, which involved the girlfriend making accusations against the Lennox boys stealing her purse.

The Culver City gang members utilized diplomacy to diffuse the situation; however, the mutual hostility had been building up. Once the first punch was thrown, it turned into a bloodbath which involved bottles, pool sticks, and liquor glasses.

The battle zone moved outside of the bar while the Culver City Police Department observed without preventing the animosity. This resulted in a Culver City gang member being shot and paralyzed, a high speed pursuit, and the incarceration and hospitalization of a few Lennox 13 gang members. The event was discussed at a Westside regional bloc Security Council meeting, which marked the end of the regional cooperation, the end of the Westside Renaissance, and the dwindling of the love and hate relationship between the Culver City and Lennox street gangs.

Although the friendly relations between Westside regional bloc gangs was severed, the Westside Renaissance rendered mega-event city status for the Westside regional bloc, specifically the Lennox, Venice, and Culver City gangs, which at least for a few years they enjoyed prestigious county-wide attention, tourism, and publicity.

CHAPTER 13: THE PROGRESSIVE MOVEMENT

In the early twentieth century, a political movement known as the Progressive Movement transformed government structures with new ideas about organization and administration. Going against the status-quo, the Progressive Movement attracted disillusioned groups and individuals who were excluded and ignored by the leadership group, which engaged in unorthodox political behavior and ideas that helped influence the reformation of government. The Progressive Movement based their philosophy on four key paradigms which included:

1. Pragmatic optimism, in which individuals succumbed to humanism and could alter the ecology of their environments.

2. Scientific management, which included budgeting and business ideas that adopted efficiency, effectiveness, and economy for organization and management.

3. An emphasis on the utilitarianism and the welfare of the citizenry, rather than cultural or religious attachments.

4. Lastly, government bureaucracies run by well-educated elites and those that have had successful achievements in business and the private sector.

The majority of progressive thinkers believed that government leadership, power, laws, and the welfare of the community could best be achieved by having those with the most knowledge, skills, and abilities perform civil duties which the average person wasn't capable of administering. The Progressive Movement transcended political parties and paradigms, but maintained that effective governance can be achieved through project development and public policy that is reflective of the citizenry, which could provide for the welfare of the community.

What resulted was the idea to constantly reinvent government organization and administration through systematic efficiency, and private-sector business practices like privatization. In the Westside regional bloc of the Los Angeles County, the Progressive Movement within certain street gangs sought to radically transform government organization and administration, but it resulted in warring factions which were directly responsible for the complete polarization of the regional bloc.

Growing up in the Westside regional bloc of the Los Angeles County in the 80's was an unconventional time for Mexican-American and other Hispanic teenagers from Santa Monica to LAX. The proximity of the ocean and the cosmopolitan neighborhoods allowed those specific teenagers to develop their faculties much more radically than their counterparts in South Central, the Valleys, the Harbor Area, or East Los Angeles.

While many individuals in the Westside lived within close proximity to the Pacific Ocean with the availability of aquatic recreation, individuals in other regional blocs only had access to the much less fluvial decadent Los Angeles River. Several residents along the Westside emerged from different socializations creating loose coalitions of disillusioned individuals due to their ecology. Many of those individuals experimented with graffiti, underground music, fashion trends, party or dance crew associations, and multiculturalism.

Nevertheless, they were also dealing with the macrocosmic problem of an ethnic identity crisis and a social paradox of existence, similar to disenfranchised teenagers growing up anywhere in the world. Several individuals who fit that prototype were known for their popular reputations around the underground community, yet conservative street gang members observed that prototype as a potential threat to their sovereignty.

Eventually, conservative street gang members' tolerance decreased, thus they coerced many individuals, pockets of individuals, or entire groups of individuals into their street gangs. All along the Westside, waves of individuals with liberal attitudes were setting the grassroots foundation for the progressive movement. Inadvertently, those liberal individuals would begin transforming status-quo norms by creating separatist cliques within the street gangs, while acquiescing and adopting cultural norms of the social contract.

158

For many of those members of the progressive movement, the transition into street gang culture functioned effortlessly because a large percentage of their constituency had prior experience with: drug experimentation, debauchery, violent behavior, enemy rivalries, vandalism, grand theft auto, and boasting attitudes. The progressive thinkers would serve as agents of change for the street gang propagandist ideology over the next few decades, specifically because they had different ideas about organization and administration, but many conservative gang members would view them as anti-patriotic or radical.

Members of the progressive movement were an elitist unit which allowed for minimal partisanship and recruitment; therefore, conservative gang members assessed their unconventional practices as intimidating. Most street gangs or cliques within the organization coveted a proliferation of membership, yet progressive thinkers viewed that as a flawed process.

The progressive thinkers believed that in order to have a strong cohesive unit, a smaller number of well-acquainted individuals was preferable than a loose coalition of divided members. They were an elitist unit that sought reformation of street gang cultural ideology, while succumbing to the urban warfare with enemy rivals. Moreover, they were not afraid of the conservative factions that existed within their street gang organization or other regional blocs; on the contrary, their elitism welcomed the conflict with open arms.

As the progressive movement began developing throughout the Westside, they began infiltrating conservative street gang norms with different ideas about organization and administration. Their unorthodox style of dress, their demographic, their positive reputations, their eclecticism, their trend-setting behavior, and their willingness to congregate in non-traditional environments attracted other groups of disillusioned individuals who preferred this prototype of unconventional street gang organization political behavior.

Due to their positive underground media attention and their reputable image which transcended convention, willing members from both the private and public sectors were eager to join the progressive movement.

However, many of those individuals did not share the progressive movement values; they were simply impressed by aesthetics. Thus, keeping true to progressive movement elitism and selection processes to maintain strict party identification, several of those willing members were rejected. What sometimes resulted were small pockets of civil unrest within certain street gangs, warring factions against enemies, and superiority over other County of Los Angeles regional blocs, all in the name of elitism and class conflict.

While progressive thinkers assimilated into street gang culture with radical political behavior, their infamous reputation throughout the underground media increased. They still worked effectively to achieve the mission statement of the social contract, but they didn't feel like they had to prove themselves to their conservative predecessors or peers.

After about a decade of being heavily involved in the political scene of street gangs, progressive thinkers were convinced that the progressive movement ideology would triumph over moderate or conservative paradigms.

In the early '90's when the general peace treaty agreement developed, it allowed progressive thinkers to pursue their unorthodox political behavior in a better sanctioned environment, while still going against the status-quo. The general peace treaty agreement took the Los Angeles County by storm, which progressive thinkers exponentially helped influence the radical transformation of the Westside regional bloc within the Westside Renaissance.

Their pragmatic optimism had already been serving street gang organizations as agents of change, but the peace treaty agreement brought them a much broader audience. Several street gangs or cliques within the organization underwent a cultural makeover, thanks to the progressive movement, which overwhelmed some on the conservative right. Immediately, many street gang organizations tried passing public policies which de-emphasized aesthetic dress, which some believed, reduced the infamous reputations of street gangs entirely.

Progressive movement values had already proved that elitist humanism within street gang organizations could alter the ecology of their environment. Progressive thinkers were naturally living proof that the ecology of their environment could assimilate to them, not the opposite. For years, progressive thinkers had been more aesthetically stylish and fashionable than their predecessors, other cliques, rival enemies, and other regional blocs, thus they dressed for ornamentation and emphasized appearance over utility, which was typical of the Parliamentary French government.

The utility factor is where the political divisions would lay, the welfare of the entire street gang or the regional bloc could not be comprehended by progressive thinkers who were heavily involved in the pursuit of capital-intensive programs. These would be the first signs of a polarized progressive movement, directly caused by class conflict.

During the Westside Renaissance, scientific management programs including: political parties, city council structures, budgeting principles, economic policies, public administration, and mega-event strategies due to the temporary deferral of urban warfare, flourished. These principles sought to achieve: efficiency, effectiveness, and economy for organizational development, all elements of the progressive movement.

Many progressive thinkers had already adopted elitism theories for several years, thus they sought to reinvent the political culture of street gang organizations through alternative methods, by running them like political structures. Several elite leaders of many street gang organizations had previously specialized in business practices in the private sector, which they could now utilize like privatization methodologies amongst the public sector of street gangs.

It was the same downfall of several popular government organizations worldwide; they could not practice utility over the welfare of the community. For many elite leaders including the progressive thinkers of street gangs, political spoils belonged to specific, experienced groups of people who had worked feverishly to maintain success.

Many progressive thinkers within street gang organizations began to emerge with a dictatorial and authoritative leadership role to assume power. Some had impressive knowledge, skills, and abilities in typical gangs because of their experience with prison congressional terms, thus they could use their trajectory advantageously to pursue leadership theory.

In 1997, there was a precedent case within the Lennox 13 street gang, in which one of these types of leaders from the progressive movement began raising skepticism amongst an insurgency group because of his information-seeking behavior. (Capone from the Night' Owls)

He was continuously gathering intelligence and empirical evidence based on logistics and operations of criminal activity through methods of extortion, extreme use of power, or physical abuse. Because of this phenomenon and other divisions of power throughout the Lennox 13 street gang, an insurgency group developed out of extreme polarization of the progressive movement within the gang.

Several of the divisions of power were directly related to distribution and collections of monies, which has always been a leading factor in the polarization of populations for numerous centuries. Coincidentally, many gang members from the progressive movement within the Lennox 13 gang and other Westside gangs were getting incarcerated for engaging in criminal activities. Most of the incarcerations seemed highly suspect because law enforcement agencies normally gather intelligence for several months or years before making big arrests, unless there was an informant.

The insurgency group within the Lennox 13 street gang had previously considered that the dictatorial leader was a federal informant, thus when a leak within the underground media reported this information as confidential and accurate, the assumption was confirmed. As the insurgent group began making military preparations for the removal of the dictator, a physical altercation between the dictator and a popular gang member from the progressive movement accelerated the agenda.

What resulted was a military coup which removed the dictator from authority by death, but two main members from the insurgency group serving out a voluntary manslaughter prison term. It engendered disillusionment of most of the street gang organization of Lennox 13, and the collapse of the Westside regional bloc. Moreover, the dictatorship was never replaced by a peaceful or democratic regime; it disenfranchised and isolated many individuals, and resulted in massive abandonment of the social contract throughout the entire Westside and civil unrest in Lennox.

EPILOGUE

The goal for many street gang organizations is to transform into an insurgent criminal organization with a political agenda that helps destabilize local law enforcement and local government to pursue their ends. Street gangs are mostly interested in local territorial concerns and petty criminal markets, however, many more sophisticated and highly developed street gangs have become organized criminal enterprises that maintain freedom of movement to pursue economic interests.

The objective could be facilitated when they establish networks of underground infrastructure, when they maintain control over certain territories that have been corrupted or are not as heavily patrolled, when they infiltrate local governments and interest groups for intelligence, political, or economic purposes to garner support, and when they establish a strong coalition with narco-traffickers that can help weaken the state, which in turn helps the destabilization of a local government.

It takes a strong, charismatic mayor-type figurehead of a street gang to consolidate the efforts to make the transition from territorial-based urban warfare, to a political agenda sought out by organized criminals. Whether the coalition is established with organized criminals or narco-traffickers is irrelevant, the street gang organization must rely on such a coalition for political reeducation to help redefine goals.

The social contract will still maintain absolute sovereignty over the individual; however, it is merely the agenda that will be redefined by the mayor-type figurehead that also transforms from petty-criminal shot-caller or mayor figurehead, to warlord or drug baron, depending on the economic interests of the street gang organization.

The destabilization of local government and law enforcement by nefarious street gangs and organized criminals weakens the legitimacy and authority of the state, contributing to the overwhelming dissatisfaction with public institutions. This will only strengthen the coalition of such underground infrastructure, and will lead to state failure, which has been the case in many parts of Latin America, Asia, and Africa, but can also be witnessed in various western regions, including the street gang capital of the County of Los Angeles.

There are already key indicators of a failing and weakened system in the greater Los Angeles region including political apathy, which demonstrates a clear message of lack of confidence in elected officials by the citizenry.

There is a lack of protection of life and private property, which in many areas of the Los Angeles County private citizens have responded with their type of protection because public officials cannot guarantee their safety in a hostile environment. In many cases there is a lack of justice because of government corruption, which was already examined with the historical timeline of the Los Angeles Police Department.

The failing public education system and the lack of affordable healthcare are also contributing factors to and leading to a failed state. Which one is only obligated to ask—is the County of Los Angeles in danger of becoming a failing regional government?

Surely with the numerous street gang organizations operating in the County of Los Angeles, who all fly under the same flag of the Sureños, it is possible to establish such working coalitions amongst each other and the infrastructure of organized criminals or narco-traffickers to directly work against local governments as a form of insurgency. If such a radical, political insurgency could develop in the County of Los Angeles, it would render the numerous local governments ineffective and inefficient, thereby allowing for the coalition to pursue its economic interests while the local government is in a period of destabilization.

Once a local government has been destabilized, or is in a weakened period of destabilization, any motivated, well-armed, and financially organized group can assume some sort of leadership and power that reduces the overall sovereignty of the state, which then becomes almost impossible to recover.

This has been the case in many regions across the globe; hence the examples of Central America and the coalition of street gang organizations and narco-traffickers throughout that region. The citizenry in those territories often view that type of coalition as a synonym of moral corruption and political scandal; in other words, they are the same players with different uniforms, but all playing the same game.

167

The government's inability to effectively provide public services and protection leads it to become a decadent regime of uncertainty where the citizens are afraid of their own elected officials because of their unofficial relationship with criminal organizations.

Many common efforts to combat such a violent phenomenon have been with military tactics. Military efforts have often been used by several failing states that can no longer maintain civil order in their society, therefore, creating a military police state to take order of uncontrollable territories. These military efforts also rely on the citizenry to provide intelligence on operations and whereabouts of resources to help combat the societal, anarchic problem of instability.

However, a much more extensive coalition can be reached with the numerous social groups that target the government as a representation of social injustice and stagnation such as: street gang organizations, organized criminals, interest groups, non-profit organizations, domestic terrorists or militias, militant environmentalists, and other such social groups that already use similar tactics of crime, terrorism, and war.

Any social group or movement that can consolidate this underground infrastructure can seriously weaken a government organization and create regional instability, thus gaining geopolitical control to develop an insurgent organization to criminally co-opt operational markets.

To understand such criminal phenomenon, one does not have to observe developing or underdeveloped countries, one could observe the Camorra criminal organization of Southern Italy in Naples and Campania. The Camorra, which is the oldest criminal organization in Italy, is a Mafia-like organization often confused with the Sicilian Mafia, whose operations are financed through drug trafficking, extortion, murder, protection, and racketeering. The Southernists' structure of the County of Los Angeles is more closely related to that of the Camorra than other criminal organizations because of their horizontal structure and independent feuds amongst separate organizations.

Simultaneously, they are both loose confederations of different independent groups that often establish coalitions to maintain power, and often the Camorra resort to drive-by shootings, territorial disputes, ruthless violence, and petty drug trafficking, also common denominators of disenfranchised communities throughout the Los Angeles County.

A significant difference between the Southernists and the Camorras is that the Camorras have a well-established presence in the undermining of political outcomes and legitimate regional industries. Just as the Camorras have established coalitions with other organized criminals, the Southernists have established coalitions with some prison gangs and organized criminals like the Nazi Low-Riders, Armenian Power, the Aryan Brotherhood, and numerous narco-trafficking organizations from Mexico in order to extend their sphere of influence.

And that is the ultimate goal of the Southernists, to destabilize the County of Los Angeles by formulating an insurgent criminal organization with a political agenda that can influence political decisions to their liking, and which can be duplicated throughout other areas of Southern California, thereby turning the city of Los Angeles into a dark metropolis.

.

Made in the USA
Las Vegas, NV
29 August 2023